Productivity Growth and the Competitiveness of the American Economy

Studies in Productivity Analysis

Editor:

Ali Dogramaci
Graduate School of Management
Rutgers University
Newark, New Jersey, U.S.A.

Previously published books in the series:

1. Dogramaci, A. and Adam, N.: *Productivity Analysis at the Organizational Level*
2. Dogramaci, A. and Adam, N.: *Aggregrate and Industry-Level Productivity Analysis*
3. Dogramaci, A.: *Productivity Analysis; A Range of Perspectives*
4. Dogramaci, A.: *Developments in Econometric Analyses of Productivity: Measurement and Modelling Issues*
5. Sudit, E.: *Productivity Based Management*
6. Fare, R., Grosskopf, S., and Lovell, C.: *The Measurement of Efficiency of Production*
7. Dogramaci, A.: *Managerial Issues in Productivity Analysis*
8. Dogramaci, A.: *Measurement Issues and Behavior of Productivity Variables*
9. Dogramaci, A., and Fare, R.: *Applications of Modern Production Theory: Efficiency and Productivity*

Productivity Growth and the Competitiveness of the American Economy

A Carolina Public Policy Conference Volume

edited by

Stanley W. Black

Kluwer Academic Publishers
Boston   Dordrecht   London

Distributors for North America:
Kluwer Academic Publishers
101 Philip Drive
Assinippi Park
Norwell, Massachusetts 02061 USA

Distributors for all other countries:
Kluwer Academic Publishers Group
Distribution Centre
Post Office Box 322
3300 AH Dordrecht, THE NETHERLANDS

Library of Congress Cataloging-in-Publication Data

Productivity growth and the competitiveness of the American economy :
  a Carolina public policy conference volume / edited by Stanley W.
  Black.
     p. cm.—(Studies in productivity analysis)
   ISBN 0-7923-9001-6
    1. Industrial productivity—United States—Congresses.
    2. Competition, International—Congresses. I. Black, Stanley W.
   II. Series.
   HC110.I52P754   1989
   338.973—dc19   88-34259
                                                                           CIP

Copyright © 1989 by Kluwer Academic Publishers

All rights reserved. No part of this publication may be reproduced, stored in a retrieval system or transmitted in any form or by any means, mechanical, photocopying, recording, or otherwise, without the prior written permission of the publisher, Kluwer Academic Publishers, 101 Philip Drive, Assinippi Park, Norwell, Massachusetts 02061.

PRINTED IN THE UNITED STATES

Contents

	About the Authors	vii
	Acknowledgements	ix
1	Economic Background and Introduction to the Papers Stanley W. Black	1
2	The U.S. Basic Industries in the 1980s: Can Fiscal Policies Explain Their Changing Competitive Position? Barry Eichengreen and Lawrence H. Goulder	9
	Comment: Robert E. Baldwin	71
3	Policy Implications of the Slowdown in U.S. Productivity Growth John W. Kendrick	75
	Comment: C.A. Knox Lovell	111
4	The Tax Reform Act of 1986 and Economic Growth Patric H. Hendershott	121
	Comment: Emil J. Sunley	151
5	A Businessman's Perspective on Competitiveness Paul J. Rizzo	155

About the Authors

Robert E. Baldwin is Hilldale Professor of Economics at the University of Wisconsin-Madison. He has written several books and numerous theoretical, empirical and policy-oriented articles in the fields of international trade and economic development. He served as Chief Economist in the Office of the U.S. Trade Representative in Washington, D.C. and as a consultant to several U.S. and International Organizations. He currently is serving as the Director of the N.B.E.R. project on U.S. Trade Relations, is a member of the Council on Foreign Relations, and is on the Advisory Committee of the Institute for International Economics.

Stanley W. Black is Georges Lurcy Professor of Economics at the University of North Carolina at Chapel Hill. He has written books and numerous articles in the area of international monetary economics and has served on the staffs of the Council of the Economic Advisors, the Board of Governors of the Federal Reserve System, and the U.S. Department of State.

Barry J. Eichengreen is Professor of Economics at the University of California-Berkeley. He has published widely in the area of international economics and international productivity and competitiveness. He has served on the faculty at Harvard University and was a member of the Federal Reserve Board in 1979. He is a member of the N.B.E.R. and the author of a recent N.B.E.R. study on U.S. productivity and international competitiveness.

Larry Goulder is an Assistant Professor of Economics at Harvard University. He has published in the international economics field and his current research concentrates on the development of general equilibrium models to investigate issues in public finance and international economics. His recent papers explore the effects of U.S. tax policies on U.S. industries' employment, profits and growth.

Patric H. Hendershott is Professor of Finance and John W. Galbreath Chairholder in Real Estate at the Ohio State University. He has well over 90 publications in the areas of monetary policy, finance, tax reform and real estate. He is currently the Editor of the AREUEA Journal, and an Associate Editor of the Journal of Money, Credit and Banking, the Journal of Financial Services, and the Housing Finance Review. He has served as a consultant to numerous government agencies and to the Federal Home Loan Bank of Cincinnati, and has written extensively on the implications of tax reform on capital formation, financial markets and housing.

John W. Kendrick is Professor of Economics at the George Washington University and adjunct Scholar at the American Enterprise Institute. He has published seven books and more than 100 articles in the area of productivity growth, trends and cycles. He has served as an economic consultant to industry and government and on the advisory committees to the Department of Commerce, the Office of Management and Budget and the National Science Foundation. In 1976-77 he was Chief Economist for the U.S. Department of Commerce and in 1972-73 he served as Vice President for Economic Research at The Conference Board. He is on the Editorial Board of the Review of Income and Wealth and is also on the Board of Directors of the Pioneer Funds of Boston and the American Productivity Center in Houston.

C. A. Knox Lovell is Professor of Economics at the University of North Carolina-Chapel Hill. He has published widely in the areas of production economics and econometrics and has collaborated on joint US-USSR research on production and cost functions and the efficiency of firms and enterprises funded by the National Science Foundation. He was a Visiting Professor at the University of Pennsylvania in 1983-84 and at the University of British Colombia in 1975-76.

Paul J. Rizzo is Dean of the Graduate School of Business Administration at UNC-Chapel Hill, and former vice chairman of IBM's Corporate Management Board, Policy Committee and Business Operations Committee. He was responsible for IBM World Trade Americas Group; IBM World Trade Asia/Pacific Group; and IBM Information Systems Group. Mr. Rizzo is a director of Burlington Industries, Inc., Johnson and Johnson, The Business Council of New York State and NACME. He is a graduate of the University of North Carolina at Chapel Hill.

Emil M. Sunley is Director of Tax Analysis in the National Affairs Office of Deloitte Haskins & Sells. He has published in the field of tax policy and is widely recognized for his expertise on income tax reform. He appears frequently before the tax writing committees of Congress, has conducted tax studies for several states and advised foreign governments on their tax reform programs. In 1977-81 he served as Deputy Assistant Secretary of the Treasury for Tax Policy. He has also served as Associate Director of the Office of Tax Analysis in the Treasury Department and as a Senior Fellow in Economic Studies in the Brookings Institution.

Acknowledgements

It is a pleasure to acknowledge the support and encouragement of the then Provost of the University of North Carolina, Samuel R. Williamson, Jr., and Assistant to the Provost C. E. Bishop. Together with a committee composed of Jack Kasarda, Edward M. Bergman, Jay Klompmaker, and Alfred Field, they supported the concept of a series of conferences on public policy topics, of which this is the first.

The conference, which was held at the Kenan Center of the University of North Carolina at Chapel Hill, could not have succeeded without the efforts of Conference Organizer Alfred Field and the assistance of Cheryl Mitchell and Kathryn Mahoney. Financial support from the Office of the Provost and from the law firm of Moore and Van Allen is gratefully acknowledged.

Productivity Growth and the Competitiveness of the American Economy

1 ECONOMIC BACKGROUND AND INTRODUCTION TO THE PAPERS

Stanley W. Black

The stock market crash of October 1987 raised basic questions about the health and future of the American economy. Can we sustain a rising standard of living if we rely on a decline in the dollar to restore our competitiveness? Do we have the right policies in place to encourage capital formation, technological change, and increased productivity?

These and other questions were debated at the first Carolina Public Policy Conference, held at the Kenan Center on the campus of the University of North Carolina at Chapel Hill on February 19, 1988. The theme of the conference was "Productivity Growth and the Competitiveness of the American Economy." It brought together a select group of leaders from the business world, academia, and government to debate the issues underlying the future of the American economy in these uncertain times.

The conference focused on the key issue of international trade, specifically, what is needed to restore the competitiveness of American industry. Three papers relating to various aspects of this question were commissioned from outstanding experts from the academic world. Well-informed discussants were asked to prepare comments on their papers. This volume presents the papers, comments by discussants, and an address given to the conference by the Dean of the Graduate School of Business at Chapel Hill. The introduction provides a background setting for the conference and an overview of the conference papers and discussion.

ECONOMIC BACKGROUND

The stock market crash of October 1987 exposed a fundamental weakness of the long-running economic expansion since 1982: its reliance on ever-increasing foreign borrowing to finance domestic investment. Expansionary fiscal policy marked by the tax cuts of 1981 and increased defense spending combined with tight monetary policies to produce a rising government deficit, draining domestic savings into government financing. In the absence of adequate domestic saving, high real interest rates and a rising dollar convinced private foreigners to lend increasing amounts to the United States, the wealthiest country in the world.

When the dollar peaked in 1985, the trade deficit had reached 3 percent of GNP; the level was of course proportionately much larger in some traditional industries. Cries for import relief, which had been earlier granted in steel and automobiles, became well-nigh irresistible, in the absence of other policy changes. And monetary policy did change in 1985, as interest rates dropped in response to slowing growth in the economy. With falling interest rates, the dollar began to drop, as foreigners could no longer expect both a high interest return on dollar assets and further increases in the value of the dollar. The Plaza Agreement of September 1985 gave an Administration seal of approval to the declining dollar, which was seen as an alternative to protection as a means to improve the trade deficit and save jobs in American industry and agriculture. The United States government began cooperating with other countries by intervening in the exchange market to nudge the dollar down.

The dollar went on falling for two years, but by early 1987 the Administration had had enough. Despite a 30 percent fall in the value of the dollar, the trade deficit had increased further, rather than declining. The problem was, there had been no change in the underlying savings-investment imbalance that had produced the trade deficit. In the Louvre Accord, it was agreed to try to stabilize the dollar by gradually tightening monetary and fiscal policy in the United States, while easing policy abroad. These policy "directions" were supplemented by substantial intervention in the exchange market to prop up the dollar, most of which was undertaken by foreign central banks, notable the West Germans and the Japanese.

During 1987, the effort to paper over the underlying payments imbalances with an agreement on exchange rates gradually fell apart. The United States found it necessary to raise interest rates to stem the fall of the dollar, threatening the onset of a recession and exposing the ever higher stock market to the unfavorable comparison of a falling bond market and rising bond yields. The Germans and the Japanese intervened heavily to prevent their currencies from rising against the dollar, and found their money supplies swollen with deutschemarks and yen newly created to purchase unwanted dollars from the markets. When the Bundesbank and the Bank of Japan began to raise <u>their</u> interest rates to slow domestic monetary expansion, the fabric of international monetary cooperation began to unravel. Amid charge and counter-charge by disgruntled finance ministers, the dollar dropped further and interest rates jumped upward, leading to panic in the stock market on Black Monday.

Fortunately, a steady hand and generous supply of credit from the Federal Reserve System prevented massive bankruptcies among Wall Street brokerage houses and a collapse of the credit system. But the world-wide reverberations of the Wall Street crash exposed the underlying weaknesses of an economy based on foreign borrowing for all to see. Furthermore, the banking system is saddled with mountains of bad debts from the Third World and depressed parts of the American economy.

A new Administration entering office in 1989 must deal with these problems, among others. Businesses and state and local governments need to know whether to focus their efforts on tax policy, investment, and improvements in education and worker training, or lobbying for protection from imports. The papers in this volume were chosen to explain the <u>causes</u> of present competitive problems in American industry and the factors that can lead to their gradual solution.

OVERVIEW OF THE PAPERS

Eichengreen and Goulder

The paper by Barry Eichengreen of the University of California at Berkeley and Lawrence Goulder of Harvard examines the experience during the 1980's of four "basic industries" of the American economy: steel, motor vehicles, textiles, and apparel. Each of these industries has faced sharply increased import penetration of their domestic markets, combined with rapid declines in output and employment. Bankruptcies, mergers, and government bailouts have become common. By 1987, these trends had begun to be reversed.

In the first section of their paper, Eichengreen and Goulder explore two sets of factors that have caused competitive problems for basic industries: private sector factors such as the international product cycle, changes in technology, productivity, labor costs, and labor relations; and government policies such as monetary and fiscal policies, the exchange rate, and trade policies.

They point out that the international product cycle dictates the development of competing suppliers in other nations for the products of the mature basic industries. In the case of steel and motor vehicles, the competing suppliers are most often in the other developed economies of the OECD countries, while for textiles and apparel they are most often in the Newly Industrialized Countries (NIC's). At the same time, the share of national spending going to steel and textiles and apparel has been declining, as incomes grow and less costly substitutes are developed.

Labor costs are relatively high in steel and motor vehicles, low in textiles and apparel. More significantly, automation by itself does not appear to be a panacea, as Eichengreen and Goulder cite evidence of difficulties encountered by General Motors with automated plants. On the other hand, the use of teamwork in production, involving greater worker participation in shop-floor decisions seems to be more beneficial. Improvements in technology are cited in the steel industry's mini-mills and plasma furnaces, the textile industry's shuttleless looms and open-end spinning rotors, and both process and product innovations in the automobile industry.

Eichengreen and Goulder next focus on movements of the exchange rate, which they describe as "the critical variable affecting the competitiveness of U.S. industry." The 80 percent rise in the value of the dollar from 1980 to early 1985 "had a profound impact on comparative domestic and foreign unit labor costs." And the 40 percent decline in the dollar to the end of 1987 helps explain the improvements in competitiveness since then. Macroeconomic policy, specifically the Reagan Administration's reliance on tax cuts, increased defense spending, and tight monetary policy in contrast with fiscal restraint abroad, is the main explanation for the movement in the dollar, although Eichengreen and Goulder find room for a speculative bubble that burst in early 1985 as well.

Trade policy, in the form of voluntary export quotas on steel, automobiles, textiles, and apparel, have not provided the protection that domestic basic industries sought, according to Eichengreen and Goulder. Instead, the sources of supply have shifted or in the case of autos the quota has become redundant due to the fall in the dollar.

The second part of Eichengreen and Goulder's paper examines the effect of the tax cuts and spending changes between 1981 and 1985 on the competitiveness of American industry, using a sophisticated simulation model of the economy embracing ten industrial sectors: agriculture and mining, crude petroleum and refining, construction, textiles and apparel, metals, machinery, motor vehicles, miscellaneous manufacturing, services, and housing. Their model ignores the effect of tight money and assumes smoothly functioning labor markets with flexible wages and a high degree of international capital mobility. Given these assumptions, they find small but deleterious effects of the Reagan fiscal policies on the competitiveness of basic industries.

In his comments on the Eichengreen-Goulder paper, Robert Baldwin noted that the small size of the simulated effects must be due to the omission of the effects of monetary tightness. He points out the political attractiveness of purchasing low inflation <u>and</u> low unemployment with a combination of tight money and loose fiscal policy. The resulting loss of competitiveness due to the high dollar is erroneously blamed on foreign countries by the public, which wants the government to respond with tough trade policies. These, Baldwin points out, may result in retaliatory barriers against U.S. exports which will make it harder to earn the foreign exchange needed to pay interest on our growing foreign debt. Baldwin also reinforces Eichengreen and Goulder's strictures against the effectiveness of trade policy, arguing that quotas against imports are both ineffective and also wasteful, since the implied tariff revenue is captured by the exporting country rather than the United States. He recommends a shift to tariffs or auctioning off the quota rights.

Kendrick

The paper by John Kendrick of George Washington University discusses the widespread productivity slowdown of the 1970's in the United States, Canada, Europe, and Japan. During the period 1950-79, the United States was a laggard in the international productivity sweepstakes, but in the 1980's productivity growth has picked up more rapidly in U.S. manufacturing industries than elsewhere.

Earlier, foreign competitors were closing a relatively large gap between productivity in the United States and other countries, saving and investing a larger proportion of their GNP to do so. No longer is there much of a gap to close. Kendrick attributes the productivity slowdown of the 1970's to slower growth of output in that troubled decade, smaller gains available to gap-closing outside the United States, and reduced levels of investment everywhere due to lower profits. The oil price shocks from OPEC were a major cause of lower profits, as workers sought to keep their wages rising faster than inflation.

Since wage rates grew relatively slower in the United States than abroad over the entire postwar period because of our lower inflation, unit labor costs in manufacturing also grew relatively slowly here, especially in the 1980's when productivity speeded up. <u>International</u> competitiveness of course depends on costs expressed in a common currency. Kendrick shows how the gradual depreciation of the dollar over the 1960's and 1970's added to the U.S. relative cost advantage, which was drastically reversed with the run-up of the dollar from 1980 to 1985. The recent decline of the dollar, by contrast, has again improved U.S. competitiveness.

After examining differences in productivity growth among industries, Kendrick discusses factors that lead to higher performance, including research and development, investment in capital equipment and the development of skills in the labor force, and economies of scale. Negative factors include wide cyclical fluctuations, unionization, strikes, and a high female share of the workforce.

With this perspective, Kendrick recommends a range of policies to improve productivity, while recognizing that the key issue of competiveness is more significantly affected by the value of the dollar. His policy recommendations focus on reduction of cyclical fluctuations, and the promotion of R&D, saving, investment, education, and training. Other factors that could help are increased involvement of workers in shopfloor decision-making and more rational regulation. Things to avoid are trade protection, a wage-price spiral, and government-directed investment choices.

In discussion, it was noted that productivity is important mainly because it is the source of higher income per capita. The trade balance depends primarily on the overall savings-investment balance (and the value of the dollar), rather than on productivity. Knox Lovell called attention to the importance of the efficiency of <u>utilization</u> of inputs, which can be measured by the gap between the best- and worst-practice firms in an industry. He argued that closing this gap could be a major source of gains in productivity.

Hendershott

Patric Hendershott of Ohio State University analyzes the effects of the Tax Reform Act of 1986 on economic growth, and therefore productivity, through its effects on labor supply, saving, and the allocation of investment. In general, he finds the effects to be negative, despite the fact the reform made the tax system fairer.

Surprisingly, Hendershott expects the tax reform to have little effect on the supply of labor by individuals, because the beneficial effects of lower tax rates are offset by other negative factors, in his view. Standard supply-side economics holds that lower tax rates will increase the supply of labor by raising the after-tax return from a given wage rate. Hendershott argues that the tax cut was financed by eliminating tax loopholes and shifting the tax burden to businesses, both of which raise prices. Elimination of loopholes raises the prices of the formerly tax-exempt activities, such as loans to buy automobiles. Raising the tax burden on business results in higher prices for consumers. These higher prices may offset the benefits of higher after-tax wages, according to Hendershott.

When it comes to saving, Hendershott notes the evidence on the response of household saving to tax incentives is contradictory. Using a broader definition of saving than is traditional, he finds the saving rate to have been approximately constant during the early 1980's, despite a massive rise in the value of the stock market. Since the increased wealth of consumers could be expected to reduce saving, Hendershott argues that its relative constancy must be due to the incentives in the 1981 tax act.

Given his belief that household saving responds to incentives, Hendershott finds that the 1986 tax reform reduced incentives for savers, on balance. On the one hand, lower tax rates raise the incentive to save. On the other hand, higher rates on capital gains, limits to passive losses, a tougher minimum tax, and less attractive IRA's reduce the incentive for households to save. Corporations will undoubtedly save less because of the increase in their tax burden. Foreigners will provide less saving to the U.S. economy if U.S. interest rates fall, as expected.

The 1986 tax reform is also negative in its effects on business investment, according to Hendershott. A modest gain in the efficiency of business investment is expected from the more equal treatment of different types of investment under the new law. But longer depreciable lives for plant and equipment and elimination of the tax credit for new business investment will reduce the overall level of investment by raising the required rate of return that must be earned to make new investment worthwhile. Hendershott estimates the overall effect of the Tax Reform Act of 1986 as a two to four percent reduction in the long run path of output.

Given his gloomy assessment of the recent tax reform, Hendershott is willing to keep the lower tax rates, improved fairness, and reduced loopholes if their effects on investment can be offset by policies to increase saving and investment. He recommends introducing a new tax on consumption to raise needed revenue, some of which could be used to increase government saving (reduce the deficit) and some to pay for a new investment tax credit.

In his comments, Emil Sunley argues that Hendershott is too negative about the 1986 tax reform. Sunley believes that the reduction in tax distortions of investment behavior will have an important effect on the efficiency of investment. Nor does he agree with Hendershott's call for a consumption tax, which he argues would have a more adverse effect on labor supply than an equivalent income tax.

Rizzo

Paul Rizzo, Dean of the Graduate School of Business at the University of North Carolina, addressed the Conference with a businessman's view of the competitiveness problem, from the background of his previous experience as vice chairman of IBM and president of IBM World Trade. His remarks focus on technological change, labor relations, and the worldwide marketplace.

2 THE U.S. BASIC INDUSTRIES IN THE 1980s: CAN FISCAL POLICIES EXPLAIN THEIR CHANGING COMPETITIVE POSITION?

Barry Eichengreen and Lawrence H. Goulder

INTRODUCTION

The first half of the 1980s was not an easy period for American industry. Following mounting difficulties in the second half of the 1970s, between 1979 and 1984 the basic industries -- steel, motor vehicles, textiles and apparel -- each experienced alarming declines in output and employment. By 1985 import penetration had reached unprecedented levels: 25 percent of domestic steel consumption, 26 percent of domestic motor vehicle sales, and 33 percent of the domestic textile market.[1] The industries' deteriorating competitive position had an immediate impact on financial performance, as reflected in declining returns on equity and widespread bankruptcy among textile and apparel firms, by rehabilitation of a financially-troubled Chrysler Corporation under the shelter of a government-guaranteed loan, and by Chapter 11 reorganization of the nation's second largest steelmaker, LTV. The persistence and severity of the difficulties led industrialists and politicians to fear for the survival of basic industry in the United States.

In the last 24 months, this situation has shown signs of reversing itself. U.S. production costs have declined to such an extent that Honda can now produce cars more cheaply in the U.S. than in Japan; the firm has begun

---

The research reported here was supported in part by a grant from the U.S. Department of Labor. We thank Erik Beecroft for excellent research assistance.

to contemplate exporting American-made autos to the Japanese market. Steel can now be produced for an estimated 18 percent less in the U.S. than in Japan.[2] In 1987, for the first time in years, the steel, automobile and textile industries all anticipated a positive return on equity, and the big three automakers registered record profits in the second quarter of 1988. Suddenly, financial distress culminating in widespread bankruptcy no longer appears to be an immediate problem. While the U.S. basic industries still have many difficulties with which to contend, they seem to be enjoying a respite from the crises of the last decade.

Businessmen and economists tend to subscribe to very different explanations for this turn of events. Businessmen emphasize the private-sector determinants of competitiveness: changes in labor relations and work organization, in labor costs, and in labor productivity. In recent years many of the basic industries have introduced ambitious programs of belt-tightening and modernization. Despite financial difficulties, each has invested significantly in new technologies and in the rationalization of existing operations. In industries such as steel and motor vehicles, where workers have traditionally earned a premium over the average manufacturing wage, management has sought and labor has agreed to a variety of wage concessions. To increase labor productivity, staffing levels have been drastically cut at both blue- and white-collar levels, and innovative work structures such as quality circles have been introduced.

Economists, in contrast, tend to emphasize government policies affecting the state of the economy and the level of the dollar as determinants of U.S. basic industry performance. Since 1980, the combination of relatively expansionary fiscal and tight monetary policies in the U.S. has tended to raise U.S. interest rates, while contractionary fiscal policies abroad have put downward pressure on foreign interest rates. The increase in U.S. interest rates relative to interest rates abroad enhanced the attractiveness of dollar-denominated assets, putting upward pressure on the U.S. exchange rate. Between 1980 and 1985, the multilateral trade-weighted value of the dollar rose by 60 percent, leading to a 25 percent fall in the dollar value of the hourly earnings of German workers at the same time that U.S. hourly earnings were rising by 35 percent in the textile industry, by 28 percent in apparel, by 24 percent in primary metals, and by 42 percent in transport equipment. With the dollar's decline since 1985, the same forces have been operating in reverse.

In 1984, Japanese and German unit labor costs in dollars were only 83 and 89 percent of those in the U.S., respectively. As a consequence of the dollar's depreciation, by 1986 they had risen to 122 and 162 percent of U.S. costs. In 1987 they were projected to rise to 142 and 193 percent, respectively.[3] These numbers illustrate vividly how exchange rate fluctuations can influence competitiveness.

A balanced analysis of the performance of the basic industries requires attention to both private-sector initiatives and government policies. In the first part of this paper, we sort through these factors and examine the ways they influence performance. Following Eichengreen (1988), we begin with an overview of recent trends and then examine several private-sector and public-policy determinants of competitiveness. In the second part of the paper, we employ a simulation model to assess the extent to which U.S. fiscal policy initiatives can explain the competitive difficulties and subsequent revival of the U.S. basic industries.

INTERNATIONAL COMPETITION IN THE PRODUCTS OF U.S. BASIC INDUSTRIES

Recent Trends

Figures 2.1 through 2.5 show trends and fluctuations in output, employment, productivity, investment and import penetration in the basic industries. A number of features of the output trends in Figure 2.1 stand out. First, output in all four industries exhibits a downward trend since the early-to-mid 1970s. Second, compared to textiles and apparel, output fluctuations in steel and automobiles are much more volatile over the business cycle, reflecting steel's status as a capital good and the automobile's status as a major consumer durable. Third, only the automobile industry has shown much tendency to make up lost ground since the early 1980s. Fourth, there is no evidence of an output recovery in 1987. In all four sectors production declined in 1986 relative to 1985. To the extent that financial performance improved, profits derive from higher prices and/or lower costs, not from increased sales.

Trends in employment, in Figure 2.2, display somewhat greater stability than the trends in output in Figure 2.1. Textile and apparel employment by now has been in slow but steady decline for decades. Recent years are notable for the relative stability of textile and apparel employment, which varied little between 1985 and 1986. The recovery of auto industry employment associated with the post-1981 economic expansion was finally halted and reversed in 1986. Employment in the steel industry is distinctive by virtue of the rapidity and persistence of its decline.

These trends combined to achieve an increase in average labor productivity, most notably in steel (Figure 2.3.)[4] Productivity growth in the steel industry is especially impressive. The 20 percent decline in industrial capacity between 1982 and 1986 was accompanied by a 51 percent reduction in the number of salaried employees. Where in 1982 the U.S. industry required more than ten manhours to ship a ton of steel, by 1986 that figure had been cut to less than seven. Part of the improvement resulted from the elimination of featherbedding, part from concentrating operations in the most efficient plants, and part from ongoing modernization and investment in new capacity.[5]

That investment behavior is shown in Figure 2.4, which depicts investment in the basic industries as a share of total manufacturing investment. Textile industry investment remains remarkably stable as a share of the manufacturing total. Auto industry investment, in contrast, displays exceptional cyclical volatility. But both series display little trend in the period since 1974. The steel industry investment share, in contrast, shows a virtually unbroken decline since the mid-1970s. In none of these industries do developments since 1985 represent a break with the recent past.

Figure 2.5 shows import penetration ratios (shares of domestic sales or apparent consumption accounted for by imports). In all three industries the upward trend in import penetration is quite dramatic -- and, from the perspective of domestic industry, alarming. Yet recent trends in import penetration have varied considerably across industries. The textile import share shows almost uninterrupted upward movement over the period, with no apparent tendency to reverse course in recent years. The same is true for apparel: in 1986, for the first time, imported apparel and fabric account for more than 50 percent of the U.S. market. Vehicle imports rise until the negotiation of voluntary restraint agreements with Japanese producers in 1981, after which they roll back at least temporarily. After 1984 they resume their upward trend. The share of imports in domestic sales of steel has fallen noticeably since 1984, with the decline of the dollar and the implementation

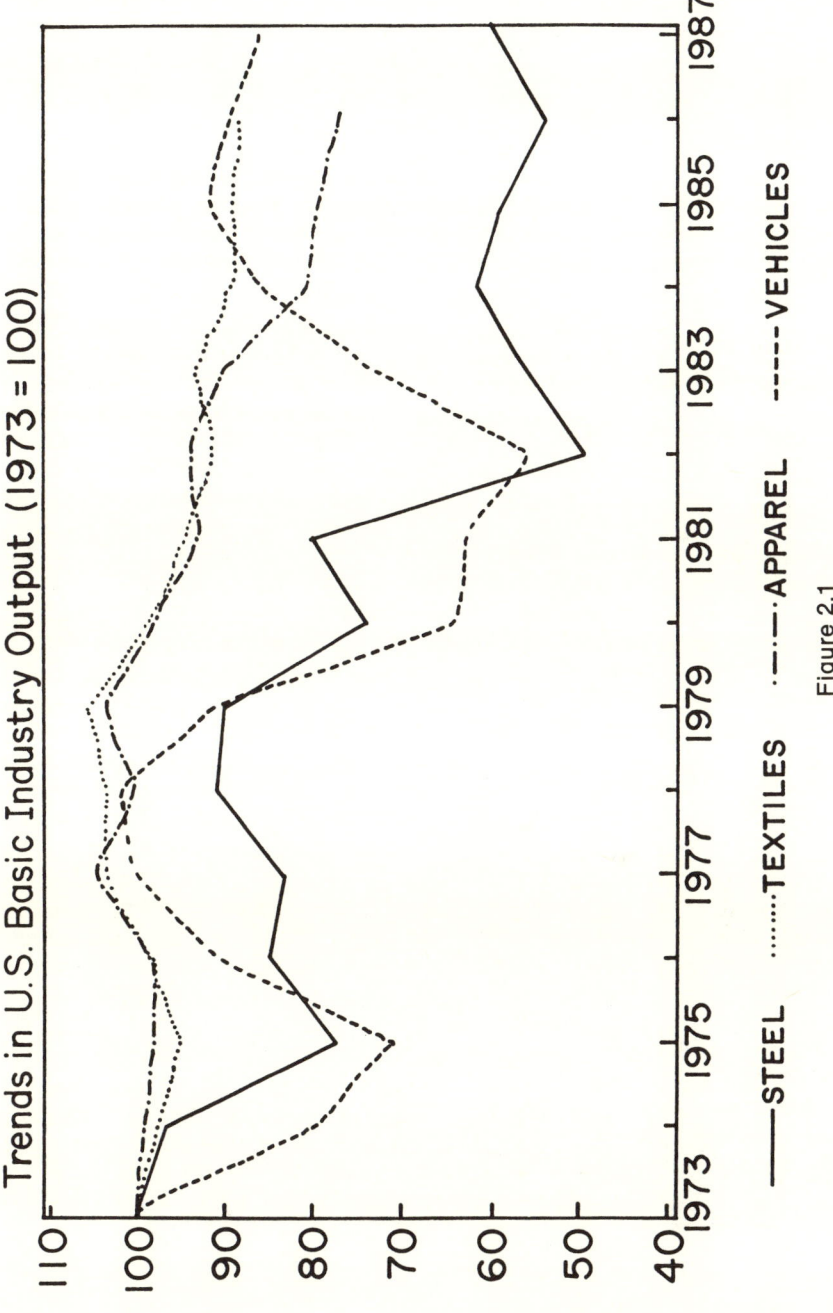

Figure 2.1

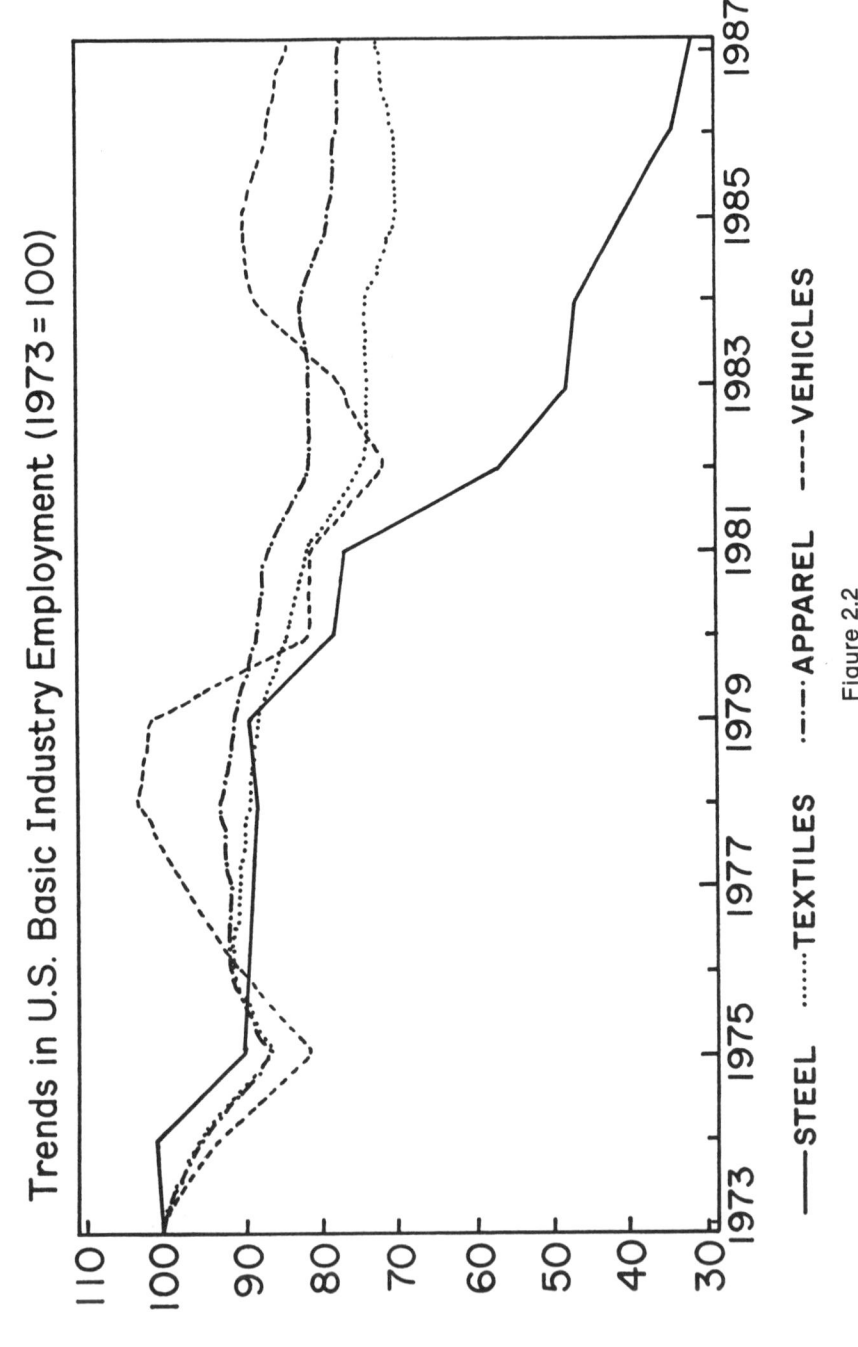

Figure 2.2

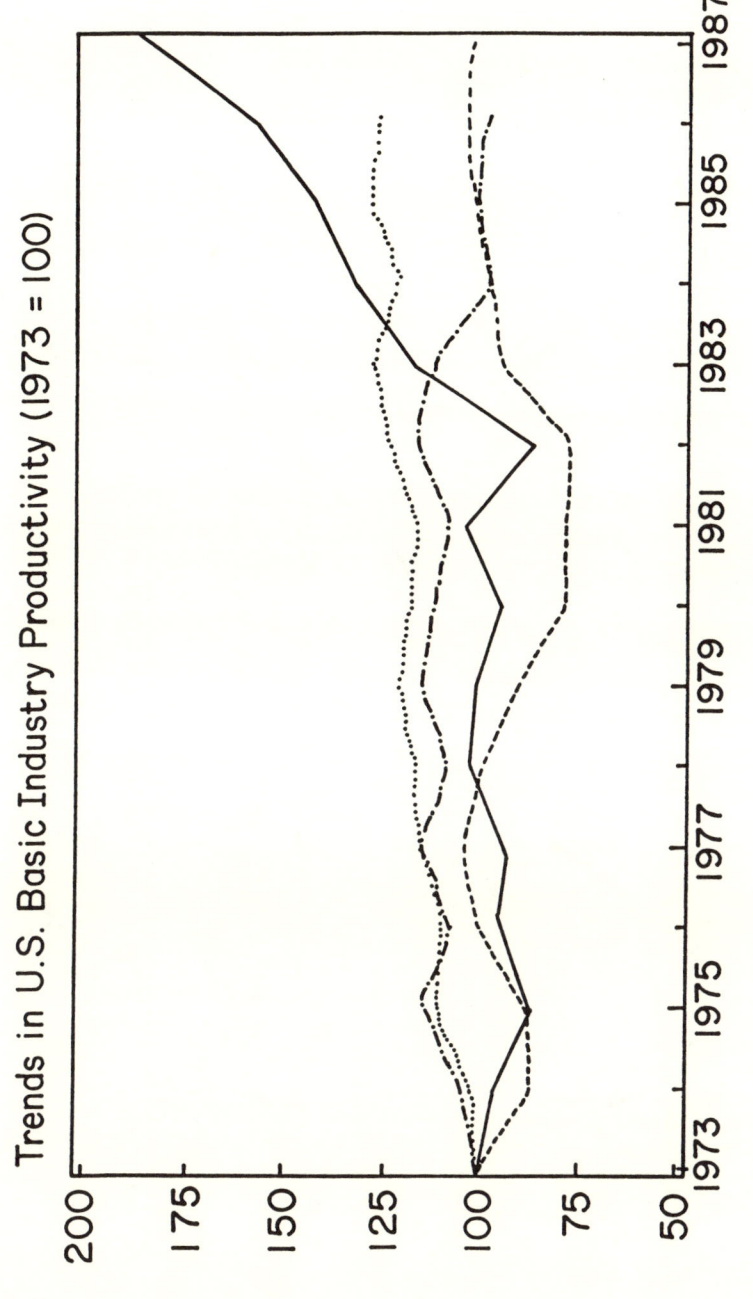

Figure 2.3

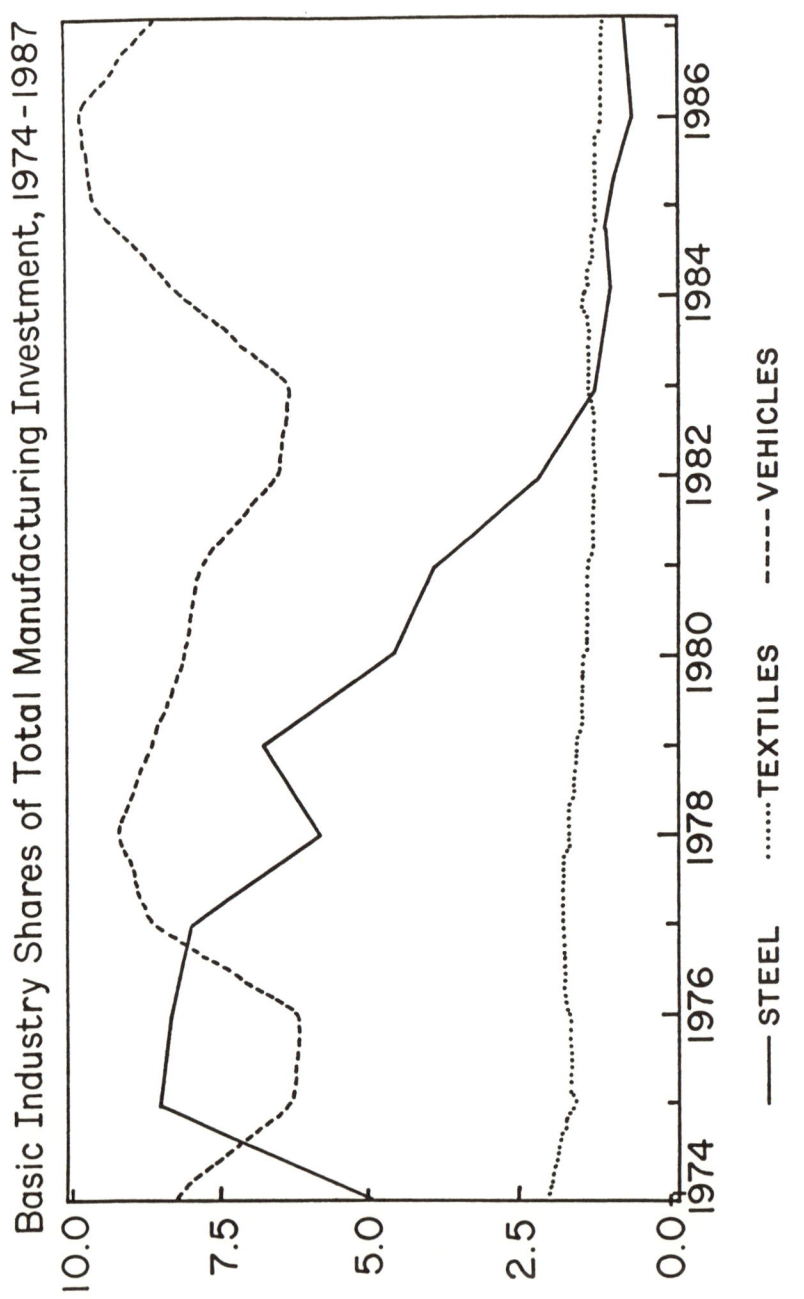

Figure 2.4

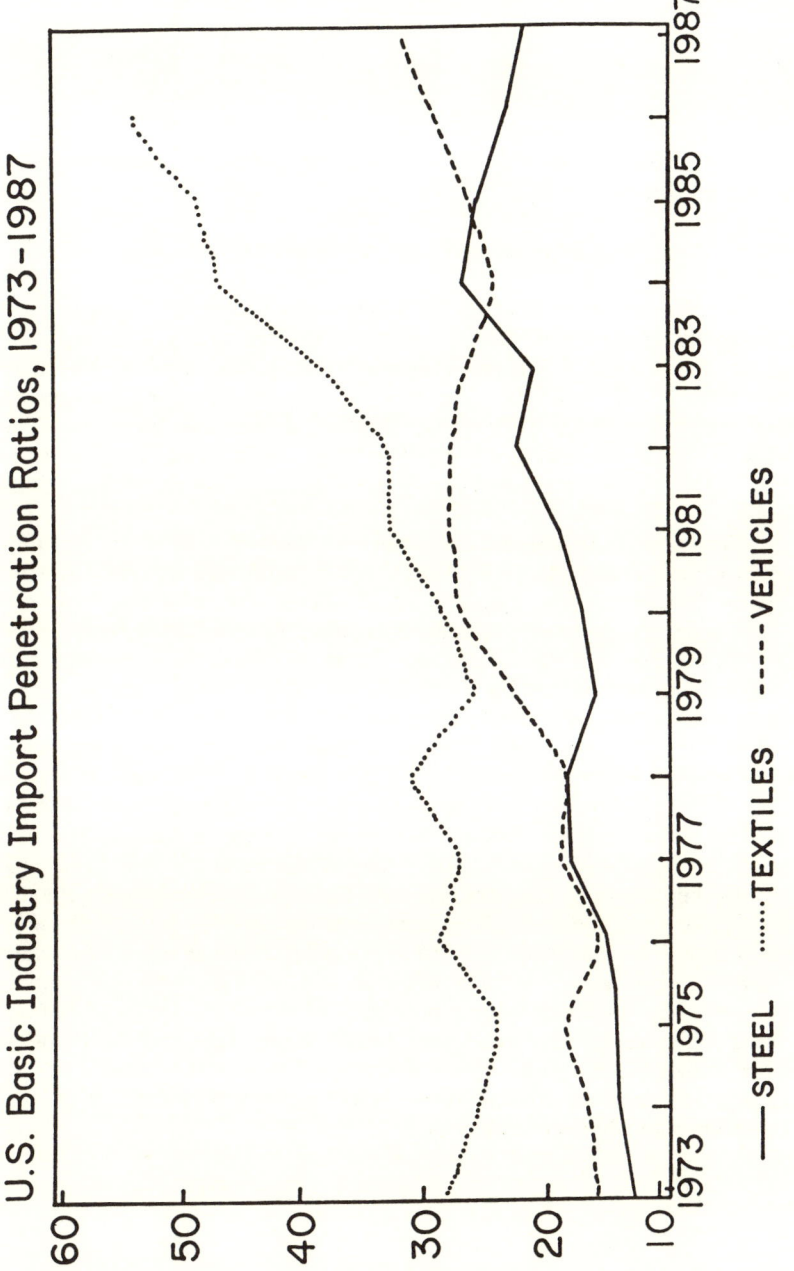

Figure 2.5

of the Reagan Administration's voluntary restraint agreements restricting sales by foreign producers.

Growth of Competing Supplies and Lagging Domestic Demand

A dominant feature of international competition in the products of the basic industries has been entry into the international arena of new national suppliers. The United States now imports textile products from more than 100 countries. Steel is sold internationally not just by Japan and Europe but by Brazil, Korea, Mexico and a host of other developing countries. The American automobile industry is bracing itself for imports not just from Europe, Japan and Korea but from Brazil, Mexico, Taiwan, Malaysia and Thailand.

While the U.S. auto and iron and steel industries continue to suffer mainly from OECD import competition, the U.S. textile and apparel industries find themselves competing mainly with the newly-industrializing countries (NICs). The impact of developing-country competition is already evident even in autos and in iron and steel, however. Table 2.1 shows the composition of U.S. vehicle imports. Notable is the rise in the share of imports from suppliers other than Japan and the major European producers, from 1/2 percent in 1985 to more than 5 percent in 1986, mainly reflecting the ready acceptance of the Korean Hyundai.[6] The trend is sure to continue: Isuzu has begun to ship its Trooper from Taiwan to the U.S.; within two years Toyota, Nissan, Fuji Heavy and Daihatsu are all expected to begin exporting cars from Taiwan; while Mitsubishi exports from Malaysia are currently slated for 1989.

In the case of textiles and apparel, the effects of developing-country competition are even clearer. The share of global capacity accounted for by the industries of the European Community and Japan has fallen dramatically. National strategies vary, but in a number of industrial countries, notably Japan, policy has encouraged the elimination of excess capacity and has not interfered with the decline in industry employment. Compared with other industrial countries, U.S. industry has maintained itself well. In contrast, the share of global capacity accounted for by the developing countries of Asia increased enormously over the period.

Table 2.1
U.S. Imports of Passenger Cars by Country of Origin, 1965-85

Year	Belgium	Canada	France	West Germany	Italy	Japan	Sweden	United Kingdom	Others	Total Imports
1986	0.2	24.8	0.2	9.6	0.2	55.8	3.2	0.6	5.3	4,691,297
1985	0.2	26.0	0.9	10.8	0.2	57.5	3.2	0.6	0.5	4,394,908
1984	0.2	22.0	5.5	8.2	0.2	55.1	2.4	0.6	5.9	4,879,560
1983	0.1	22.8	5.8	9.0	0.1	57.6	3.0	1.5	0.1	3,667,023
1982	0.1	22.9	2.9	11.0	0.3	59.4	2.5	0.4	0.1	3,066,992
1981	0.1	18.8	1.4	12.6	0.7	63.7	2.3	0.4	0.1	2,998,561
1980	0.1	18.3	1.5	14.5	1.4	61.3	1.9	1.0	0.1	3,248,266
1979	0.1	22.5	0.9	16.4	2.4	53.8	2.2	1.6	0.1	3,005,523
1975	1.8	35.4	0.8	17.8	4.9	33.5	2.5	3.2	0.1	2,074,653
1970	2.5	34.4	1.8	33.5	2.1	18.9	2.9	3.8	0.1	2,013,420
1965	0.1	5.2	4.5	67.3	1.7	4.6	4.6	11.9	0.1	559,430

Note: Percentages may not add to 100 due to rounding.

[a] Number of vehicles.

Source: Calculated from Motor Vehicle Manufacturers Association, MVMA Facts and Figures, 1985

U.S. basic industries have suffered serious difficulties because they have been caught in a squeeze between this growth of competing supplies and lagging domestic demand. The share of domestic spending devoted to the products of each of the basic industries has been in steady decline for decades. Domestic steel consumption as a share of GNP has declined most dramatically, especially after 1972. Common explanations include the tendency of the steel intensity of production to fall as the economy matures, and the development of increasingly attractive steel substitutes such as the plastic and concrete tubing used in construction, the aluminum and plastic used in the production of food and beverage containers, and the plastics used in automobile production. Similarly, U.S. consumer expenditure on clothing and shoes as a share of GNP has been in steady decline, from more than nine percent in 1960 to less than seven percent in recent years. The common explanation is that the income elasticity of demand for apparel is less than unity. Motor vehicle apparent consumption as a share of GNP has been the most stable, declining only marginally over the last two decades.

One way out of this squeeze is to export basic-industry products. To date, exports have been minimal. Exports of steel products account for a mere one percent of U.S. production, although there is some prospect that, with the dollar's fall, this share will increase (U.S. export tonage rose from 929,000 tons in 1985 to 1.1 million tons in 1987).[7] Exports of transport equipment are similarly slight, although there is evidence of change: Honda has begun to export motorcycles from its Marysville, Ohio plant and to use the U.S. rather than Japan as the source of autos sold in Taiwan and South Korea; Honda, Mazda and the Big 3 U.S. automakers all are considering the export of cars from their U.S. plants to Japan, while Chrysler is laying plans to export cars to Europe. Overall, U.S. vehicle exports rose by more than eight percent between 1986 and 1987.

Labor Costs, Labor Productivity and Work Organization

Relative costs of production are a leading determinant of how much of this limited market is captured by American producers. Much of the debate over the international competitiveness of U.S. basic industries revolves around labor costs and labor productivity. Figure 2.6 shows trends over the last two decades in the average hourly earnings of employees in the U.S. basic

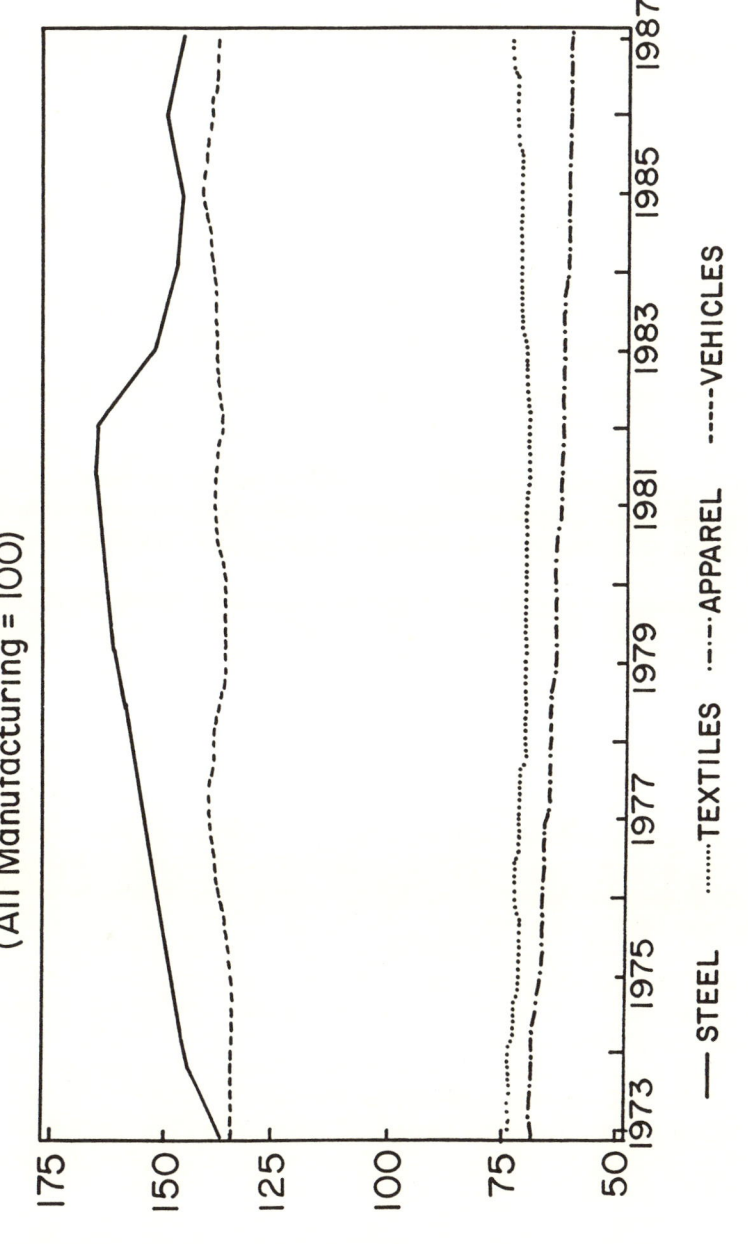

Figure 2.6

industries relative to all manufacturing employees. The contrast between high-wage steel and autos and low-wage textiles and apparel is striking.

Textile and apparel industry wages are less than 75 percent of the manufacturing average and trend slowly downward over the period. Steel and auto industry wages are more than 125 percent the manufacturing average and trend upward until the early 1980s. Earnings in steel then decline sharply as the industry's difficulties mount after 1982; in contrast, auto industry wages show little movement relative to the manufacturing average.

It is in steel that recent developments represent the most dramatic break with the past. The trend continues: in February 1987 the United Steel Workers' membership took an eight percent pay cut following a six-month strike against USX. The new contract, which runs for four years, reduces the company's labor costs by about $2.50 an hour, with $2 to be restored by 1991. For its part, USX agreed to modernize several plants previously considered candidates for closure, to limit the extent of outsourcing, and to provide profit sharing.[8]

What is not evident in Figure 2.6 is an explanation for the recent turnabout in the competitiveness of U.S. autos and steel. For years, auto and steel industry executives argued that the difficulties experienced by these sectors were due in considerable measure to the high wages they were forced to pay relative to other manufacturing industries. Despite steps in the direction of wage moderation, there is no evidence of dramatic developments on the wage front post 1984 that can help explain the steel and auto industries' return to profitability. If the source of the steel and auto industries' recovery lies here, it must be found in the relative cost of domestic and foreign labor (due to exchange rate changes and other factors considered below) or to changes in the productivity of U.S. labor due to changes in work organization and technology.

The auto industry's initial response to competitive difficulties was to emphasize technology. As epitomized by the strategy adopted by General Motors in 1979, the idea was to rely on computers and robots to achieve a reduction in unit labor costs. In the succeeding eight years, GM spent some $60 billion on plant, equipment and vehicle design. Many of the high-tech plants have had nagging problems, as epitomized by GM's well-publicized difficulties with its showcase Buick City complex in Flint, Michigan. The failure of the technology-intensive strategy is now widely blamed for GM's loss of market share and for the lag in its labor productivity compared to Ford.

One alternative to the technological solution is innovative forms of work organization and management: quality circles, team production and Japanese management styles. GM is now a leader in this counterrevolution: its joint venture with Toyota, New United Motor Manufacturing (NUMMI), in Fremont, California is the best-known example of the Japanese approach. Workers in Fremont are organized into teams possessing unprecedented control over their jobs. Only four job classifications are distinguished. As of the summer of 1986, this plant used only 8 percent more labor hours than its highly efficient sister plant in Japan and only half the labor hours that had been required when the plant was under GM's sole management, despite the fact that NUMMI makes use of considerably less automation than the average U.S. auto plant. Quality generally exceeds the best from GM's most highly automated factories.[7]

In light of this astonishing performance, GM plans to install teams in all of its plants. In the first half of 1987, more than 30 GM assembly plants sent managers and UAW officers to study NUMMI. GM's gigantic Saturn plant in Tennessee plant will have only five job classifications and will refer to workers as partners. Conversely, because workers at GM's Norwood, Ohio plant were unwilling to accept teams, the company chose to close Norwood and maintain its Van Nuys, California plant despite that the two factories produced the same car and Norwood made them for some $600 less.

In the steel industry, although the scope for team production may be more limited, but the same trend is evident. When Rouge Steel recently opened a new continuous caster, transferring workers there from existing operations, the union agreed to a major compression of job classifications.[10] Several steel firms and the United Steel Workers have received training grants from the U.S. Department of Labor to teach participation techniques. The success of these programs led to the formation of a joint planning committee to continue the process.

More typical of the steel industry than quality circles are incentive pay and profit sharing. Birmingham Steel Corp. has had success with a productivity enhancement scheme which uses pay incentives tied to productivity. Starting with nonunion workers and a base pay of $8 an hour, employees can earn up to 150 percent more in supplements. Workers who are 30 minutes late for their shift lose that day's incentive pay. Those who miss a day of work for any reason other than a death in the family lose their bonus for the week. The lost bonus money is split among members of the production unit receiving incentives. Executives claim that the scheme is responsible for Birmingham Steel's emergence as one of the lowest cost steel producers in America.[11]

As the example of GM's Norwood and Van Nuys factories reveals, labor sometimes opposes the introduction of teams. Another example of this phenomenon occurred in the fall of 1986, when GM asked workers at its Pontiac, Michigan truck and bus plant to accept a Japanese-style production system. When union leaders rejected teams but GM attempted to implement them nonetheless, a four day strike ensured. Reasons for worker reisstance vary. Some workers object that management is moving too quickly to modify established conventions. Others suspect that teams are simply a device to get them to work harder. Labor leaders sometimes resist simplications of work rules and job classifications which reduce union control over the production process. For their part, lower-level managers can be reluctant to give up traditional powers.

The employer response is to offer incentives for the acceptance of team production or to link acceptance to other decisions affecting job security. In the case of the Pontiac, Michigan factory cited above, GM offered to make the plant the source of a new truck to be added to the company's line. Company-wide agreements negotiated in the fall of 1987 between the UAW and GM and Ford include employment security guarantees, under which workers can be laid off only as a consequence of auto sales declines. To obtain these guarantees, workers declared a willingness to accept work practice changes. Other provisions of the agreements provide for plant-level committees of workers and supervisors to hammer out changes in work rules. Chrysler and the UAW have similarly negotiated plant-level agreements that permit teamwork and reduce job classifications.[12]

Katz et al. (1987) surveyed work practices and productivity in 53 plants of one of the major U.S. auto manufacturers. They employed two proxies for labor efficiency: number of production-worker labor hours per vehicle in final vehicle assembly plants, and number of supervisors per production worker.[13] The authors regress these dependent variables on measures of the flexibility of work rules, the extent of worker participation in shop-floor decisions, plant wages relative to wages in the local labor market, the unemployment rate in the local labor market, and the plant-specific absentee rate. They find that the extent of participation in shop-floor decisions consistently displays a negative association with labor hours required per unit of output, although the statistical significance of the correlation varies. Surprisingly, the presence of teams by itself appears to have a negative impact on productivity. It seems that worker participation in decision making rather than a particular organization of labor input has done most to enhance productivity. Moreover, Katz et al.'s findings serve as a warning that team methods, when introduced with inadequate preparation, may be counterproductive.[14]

Macroeconomic Policy and the Real Exchange Rate

Over the decade of the 1980s, the exchange rate has emerged as perhaps the critical variable affecting the international competitiveness of U.S. industry. Between 1981 and 1985, the multilateral trade-weighted value of the dollar rose by more than 60 percent against foreign currencies. The conventional explanation for the dollar's rise stresses the U.S. macro-policy mix. The mechanism is as follows. The budget deficits experienced under the Reagan Administration increased domestic aggregate demand. Excess demand for traded goods could be satisfied by importing them from abroad -- in other words, by running trade deficits. But the demand for nontraded goods like housing and certain services had to be rationed by increasing their relative price; hence a rise in the dollar was needed to switch expenditure away from nontraded goods and toward now cheaper imports. The mechanism can also be viewed from the perspective of U.S. savings and U.S. investment. Budget deficits imply a decline in national saving relative to national investment (assuming no offsetting rise in private saving). The demand for limited liquidity drives up U.S. interest rates, making investment in the United States increasingly attractive to foreigners. The dual result is a capital inflow as foreigners fill the gap between domestic savings and domestic investment, and a rise in the exchange rate as foreigners bid for dollar-denominated assets. Thus, dollar appreciation was the result of domestic policies elevating the level of U.S. real interest rates relative to those prevailing abroad.

Through the beginning of 1984, this conventional story helps to explain the dollar's rise, especially when augmented with the effects of restrictive monetary policy at home and tight fiscal policy abroad. But between 1984 and its 1985 peak, the dollar continued to rise at rates that cannot be explained by the real interest rate differential between the United States and abroad (Hooper and Mann, 1987, pp. 51-52). The failure of real interest differentials to explain this portion of the dollar's rise led some economists to characterize it as a speculative bubble: like Wall Street speculators, foreign-currency traders in their optimism bought the dollar in expectation of its continued rise simply because they thought others would do the same (Frankel and Froot, 1987). The dollar's collapse since the summer of 1985 reflects partly the bursting of this bubble, partly deficit-reduction initiatives in the U.S. along with increased government spending abroad (notably in Japan), partly more expansionary U.S. monetary policy, and partly the growth of debt to foreigners that must be serviced.

These exchange rate swings have had a profound impact on comparative domestic and foreign unit labor costs. Figure 2.7 shows indices of German and Japanese earnings translated into dollars. Both indices but German labor costs in particular show dramatic downward movement in the period of dollar appreciation after 1980. German labor costs in dollar terms decline by more than 20 percent over the first half of the 1980s, a period during which U.S. labor costs rose by roughly 33 percent due to wage inflation. It is easy to see how swings of this magnitude could pose serious problems for German industry's American competitors. As the dollar begins to fall in 1985, the dollar value of foreign labor costs rises dramatically. The near doubling of the dollar value of rest-of-OECD labor costs between their 1984-85 trough and early 1987 could do much to relieve the competitive pressures faced by U.S. industry.

To pinpoint the effect of exchange rate changes on labor costs, the dollar value of earnings should be adjusted for changes in labor productivity. Recent estimates of comparative unit labor costs in dollars, which make this adjustment (Table 2.3) only reinforce the conclusion derived from simple earnings comparisons. Throughout Europe, the dollar value of labor costs falls very dramatically during the period of dollar appreciation (taken here as 1980-84). As the dollar reverses field, relative foreign unit labor costs in dollar terms rise equally dramatically, more than doubling in the case of Germany.

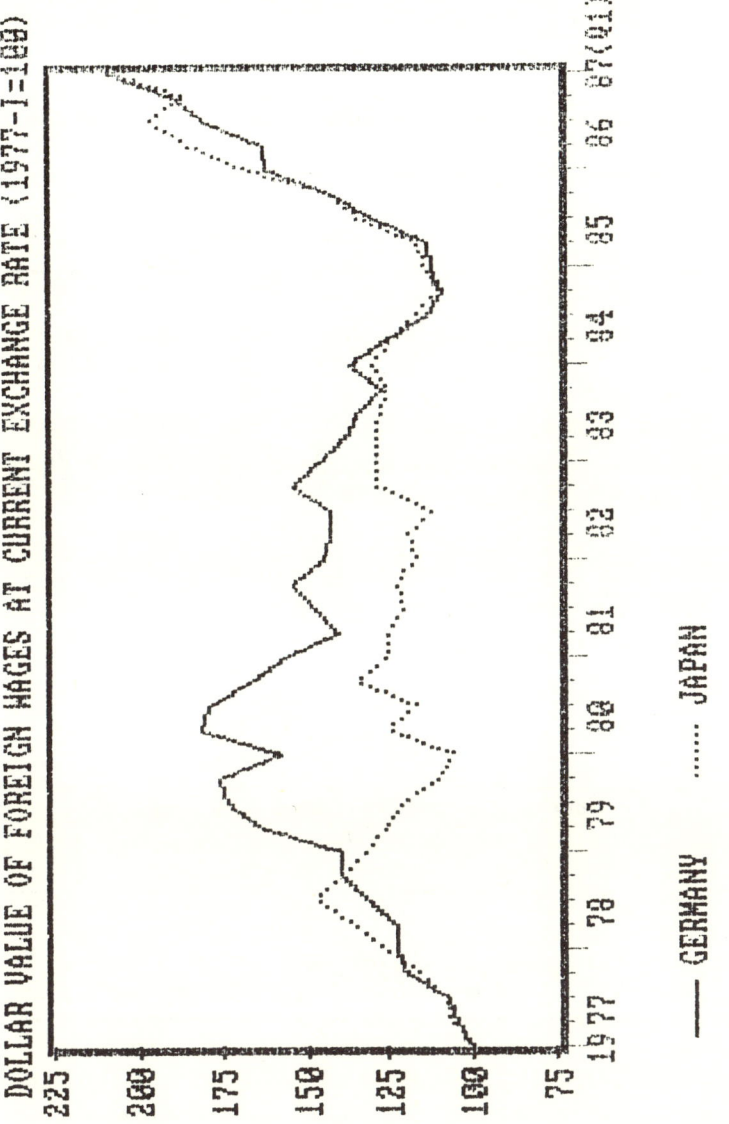

Figure 2.7

Table 2.2

Relative Unit Labor Cost Indices in Dollar Terms (U.S. = 100)

	1980	1984	1986	1987*
US	100.0	100.0	100.0	100.0
Japan	89.1	83.3	121.6	142.4
W. Germany	141.3	88.7	161.7	193.3
France	137.0	86.0	110.0	118.2
Italy	134.8	100.8	136.7	153.9
UK	217.3	135.1	166.6	185.1

*1987 calculated as 1986 unit labor costs updated with 1987 currency values as of June 10, 1987.

Source: National Institute of Economic and Social Research, press release, June 1987.

Table 2.3

International Comparison of Input Costs, Steel, 1982
(in dollars)

	Labor	Coking Coal & Iron Ore	Energy	Total	Diff. from US
US	234	103	72	409	0
EEC	113	100	62	275	-134
Japan	85	90	64	239	-170
Brazil	80	95	65	240	-169
S. Korea	37	90	66	193	-216

Source: Mueller (1985).

The paradox is that these swings in exchange rates and labor costs have not had a greater impact on U.S. import prices. Despite the dollar's dramatic fall in 1987, U.S. semifinished steel prices rose by no more than 5.2 percent over the calendar year.[15] Figure 2.8 juxtaposes the indices of the dollar value of German and Japanese earnings from Figure 2.7 with indices of the prices of U.S. imports of steel, autos and motor vehicles. Since 1984, import prices have risen very little compared to the dollar value of German and Japanese wages. Only in the case of motor vehicles is the upward trend in n import prices pronounced.

Various explanations can be offered. First, the dollar has fallen much further against the currencies of America's OECD trading partners, such as Germany and Japan, than against the currencies of the South Asian NICs (see Cox, 1986; Feldstein and Bachetta, 1987).[16] Since auto imports are drawn from Japan and Europe while textile imports are drawn primarily from the NICs, it follows that vehicle prices should have risen more dramatically than textile prices. Another explanation cites efforts on the part of foreign suppliers to defend their market shares.[17] Rather than alienate their long-standing customers, foreign producers may hesitate to quickly alter prices inresponse to exchange-rate swings, preferring to absorb the short-run effects in profits. Insofar as they similarly had hesitated to lower their export prices during the period of dollar appreciation, foreign suppliers might view the dollar's subsequent depreciation as simply bringing their costs and prices back into line, and therefore as requiring no change in prices.

Moreover, a portion of foreign production costs is affected by exchange rate swings. The dollar cost of energy and other commodity prices quoted in dollars is unaffected by swings in the U.S. exchange rate. The importance of this factor is evident in Table 2.3, on comparative steel production costs. For Japan, which imports its energy, 27 percent of variable costs are dollar denominated. For Europe, the comparable figure is 36 percent. Holding labor costs fixed, we would anticipate that a change in the dollar/yen exchange rate would change the dollar marginal cost of Japanese steel production by less than 3/4 of the value of the dollar/yen swing, for Europe by less than 2/3. For this energy-intensive basic industry, there is good reason to anticipate that exchange-rate pass through would be less than one for one.

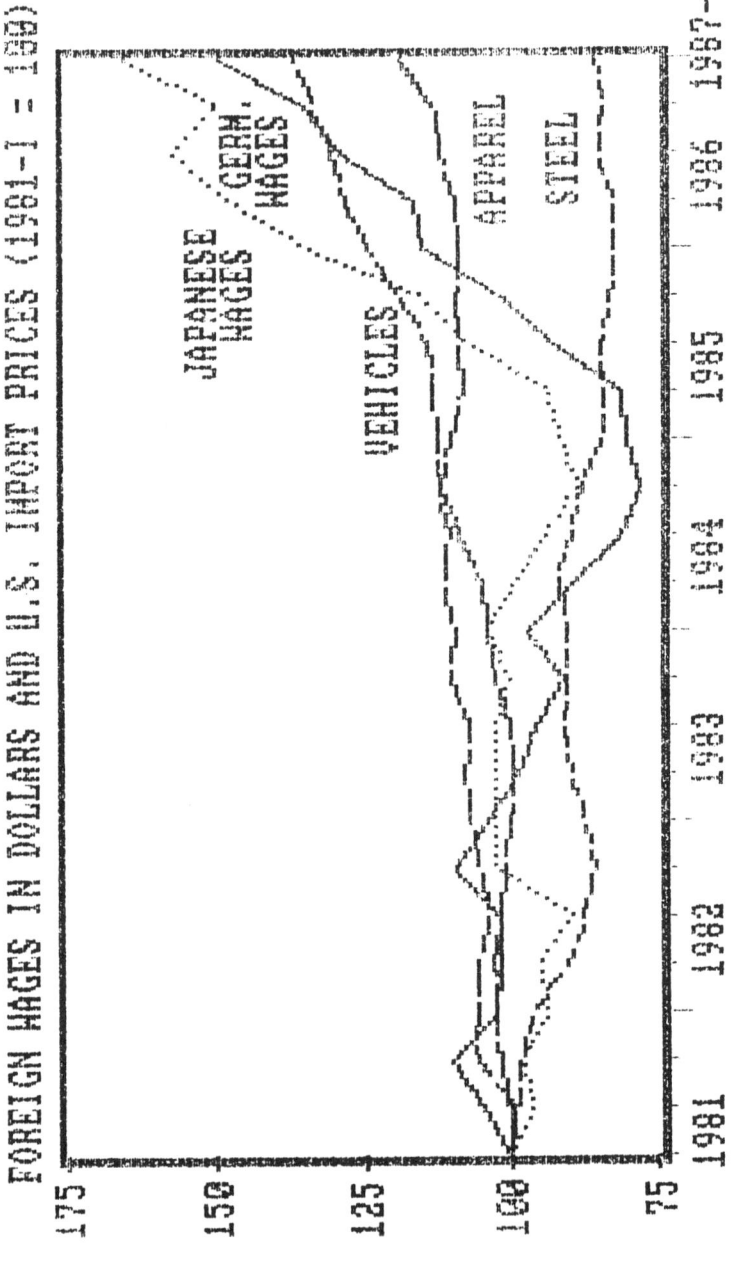

Figure 2.8

It is likely that all of these factors have contributed at least to some extent to the stability of U.S. import prices in the face of a steadily declining dollar. The problem for analysts is not a scarcity of explanations but that the recent behavior of import prices represents something of a break with the past. These same explanations presumably applied in previous periods of dollar fluctuation. Yet standard equations which successfully predicted previous movements in import prices and quantities are less successful in predicting recent movements in U.S. import prices and quantities (see Krugman and Baldwin, 1987; Mann, 1986; Hooper and Mann, 1987).

Despite the relative stability of import prices, exchange rate swings can still have a pronounced impact on the export side. The textile and apparel industries provide a case in point. Exports of apparel had been increasing since 1971. But in 1982, with the dollar's rise, they dropped abruptly by a quarter. A similar phenomenon is observable in textile exports which, having risen since 1976, fell by 24 percent in 1981.[18]

Trade Policy

The competitive position of the U.S. basic industries has been significantly affected by changes in tariff and nontariff barriers to U.S. imports of competing products.

Voluntary restraint agreements with foreign textile producers first negotiated in the 1930s have been maintained ever since. The present arrangement, known as the Multifiber Agreement (MFA), was first concluded as part of the 1973 GATT round of negotiations. Where previous agreements had encompassed only certain countries and products, which encouraged developing countries to shift out of the production of restrained items such as cotton textiles into unrestrained man-made fibers and apparel, the MFA was designed to be comprehensive. Governments were permitted to impose unilateral import controls in the event of "market disruption" (defined as serious damage to the domestic industry) and to negotiate lower rates of

Table 2.4

U.S. Domestic Consumption: Steel Mill Products
(Million Tons)

	1972	1977	1982	1987
GNP (Bil 1982$)	2,560	2,959	3,166	3,788
M Tons/Bil 1982$	41.6	36.6	24.9	24.9
Total Steel Mill Product Consumption	106.5	108.4	76.6	94.5
Integrated Mill Shipments	82.7	80.9	50.1	57.4
Mini-Mill Shipments	5.6	8.2	9.1	16.4
Domestic Shipments	88.3	89.1	59.2	73.8
Imports	18.2	19.3	17.4	20.7
Total	106.5	108.4	76.6	94.5
MARKET SHARES (%)				
Integrated Mills	77.6	74.6	65.4	60.7
Mini-Mills	5.3	7.6	11.9	17.4
Domestic Shipments	82.9	82.2	77.3	78.1
Imports	17.1	17.8	22.7	21.9
Total	100.0	100.0	100.0	100.0

Source: "Steel Markets and Mini-Mills", Study 3301, by Milos Markovic, Leading Edge Reports, Cleveland. Cited in 33 Metal Producing (March 1988), p. 21.

import growth for items upon which domestic producers were particularly dependent. Quotas were established through the negotiation of bilateral agreements covering more than 80 percent of U.S. textile and apparel imports. For example, the MFA initially restricted the growth of textile imports from Japan to five percent annually and from Taiwan, Hong Kong, South Korea and Malaysia to 7 - 7 1/2 percent per annum. New entrants and small suppliers were treated more leniently.

Increasingly, the source of U.S. textile imports has shifted from Japan and Europe to Asia, notably Hong Kong, Taiwan, South Korea and China, which currently supply about half of U.S. textile imports. This shift has been accompanied by a surge in import penetration: import growth averaged 15 percent per annum between 1981 and 1985. Several factors contributed: the bilateral agreement with the People's Republic of China permitted quota growth of 10 percent per annum; the NICs shifted resources into the production of those few goods still not under quota; and production shifted to countries such as Sri Lanka and Mauritius for which quotas did not exist. The sharp appreciation of the dollar after 1981 heightened the incentive for foreign exporters to respond in these and other ways.

At the end of 1983, under intense industry pressure, the Reagan Administration moved to establish 300 new textile quotas and to tighten enforcement. Despite the fact that the rate of growth of textile imports fell to less than seven percent in 1985, pressure from the industry led Congress to pass a restrictive textile quota bill in 1986 and to attempt to override the President's veto, compelling the Administration to negotiate preemptive agreements with Korea, Taiwan and Hong Kong. These limited import growth to approximately one percent per annum compared to nearly nine percent from 1981 to 1984, and extended coverage to silk blends, ramie and linen, fibers into which foreign producers have moved in response to previous restrictions.

A new restraint agreement with China, now the leading supplier of textiles to the U.S., proved more difficult to conclude. Textile exports are the main source of foreign exchange earnings for the Chinese, who also may be less sensitive to U.S. political pressures than the Koreans and Taiwanese. The result of these negotiations was only announced on December 19, 1987.[19] Under the provisions of this agreement, to run from 1988 through 1991, the growth rate of China's exports will be cut to three percent from their 19 percent average since mid-1983.

Steel imports have been regulated in similar fashion. A distinguishing characteristic of steel quotas is their definition in terms of market shares.

European producers agreed to restrain their U.S. sales to specific shares of U.S. apparent consumption. VRAs were negotiated with other major suppliers including Japan, Mexico, Brazil and South Africa, by the end of 1985 covering some 80 percent of the U.S. market. These agreements were designed to reduce the import share of domestic sales from the 25.2 percent reached in 1985 to no more than 20.5 percent. On coming into full effect in calendar year 1986, they reduced the import share to 23.0 percent. This was a significant drop, albeit one smaller than anticipated as a result of quota-induced shifts among product categories and suppliers.

Explicit VRAs on vehicle imports are a relatively recent phenomenon. Japan first agreed to restrain car exports in the year beginning April 1, 1981 by limiting their rate of growth to 7.7 percent. The increase in Japanese exports was held at this level for two subsequent years, after which the ceiling was raised by 10 percent. Since 1985 MITI has continued to regulate automobile exports unilaterally rather than through agreements negotiated with U.S. authorities. In the fiscal year ending March 31, 1987, it restricted exports to the U.S. to 2.3 million units. In the next fiscal year the rate of decline of the dollar rendered the restraints largely redundant. The dollar's depreciation led Japanese automakers to raise their prices significantly, cutting into their sales. As of early 1988, Japanese exports are running at a rate of two million units a year, some 300,000 below restraint limits. Dealers agreed, however, to take their entire quota of passenger cars and hold them in inventory to prevent MITI from reducing their allocation for the coming year. Ultimately, MITI agreed to retain the 2.3 million quota for another fiscal year.

Even if MITI's administrative guidance no longer affects the industry as a whole, it continues to affect individual producers. Daihatsu launched U.S. sales on December 1, 1987 with a binding quota of a mere 11,498 cars through March 31, 1988. It may be able to circumvent restrictions by exporting not from Japan but from its overseas plant in Taiwan, as may Nissan and Subaru. Although labor cost differentials play a role, the likelihood of an increasing Taiwanese presence in the U.S. market also has been stimulated indirectly by U.S. quotas on Japanese exports and by MITI administrative guidance of the same.

Another factor contributing to the redundancy of the VRA is the growth of Japanese production on U.S. soil. Sales of Hondas, Toyotas and other Japanese vehicles assembled in North America take place partly at the expense of imports of the same brands, although whether the "crowding out" is one for one or considerably less is a matter of dispute. Donald E. Petersen, chairman of Ford, in October 1987 created a stir in Japan when he suggested that the import limit be cut by 600,000 cars for the fiscal year beginning April 1, 1988. His reasoning was that Japanese-owned plants in the U.S. would produce 1.2 million cars in that period, and since about 50 percent of their parts come from Japan they are equivalent to 600,000 imports.

Most standard rationales for protection do not provide a justification for reducing imports on the grounds that foreign suppliers have set up domestic plants. One standard, albeit controversial argument for protection is to defend industry employment because employees possess skills that are not easily transferred to other sectors. This argument provides no grounds for additional restrictions on imports, since the growth of "transplants," as these migrant factories are called, only transfers employment among domestic auto plants. The standard infant-industry argument for protection -- that domestic automakers require only temporary protection to get up to Japanese standards -- has limited applicability to an industry now nearly a century old. The argument that the industry now requires protection to adjust to changing market conditions is undermined by the fact that it has now enjoyed such protection since 1981 and that it is already turning profits. Only the controversial national defense argument, that U.S. security necessitates U.S. automakers, and special compassion for the plight of auto company executives and shareholders would seem to justify such measures.

New Technology

In steel, the most important technological development of recent years has been the mini-mill.[20] Mini-mills use electric furnaces, in conjunction with continuous casters and a rolling mill, in contrast to integrated mills that rely traditionally on basic oxygen furnaces. In the basic oxygen furnace, iron ore is charged into a furnace together with coke. (The ore may be pre-treated, either by being concentrated into pellets or by being cooked with the coke into sinter.) The blast furnace produces pig iron, which is raw iron with impurities such as excess carbon. The pig iron is poured into an oxygen converter, together with scrap, and oxygen is blown into the mixture, which removes the impurities. Finally, alloying elements are added and liquid steel is cast. In the electric arc furnace, in contrast, steel scrap is melted, impurities are removed and liquid steel is cast all in a single step. Since most electric furnaces use scrap as their raw material, they require no equivalent of the blast furnace. As a result, 50 mini-mills can be constructed for a fraction of the capital cost of an integrated mill.

Mini-mill firms have additional cost advantages. Only a minority are organized by the USWA. The unionized minority pay relatively low wages and operate under more flexible work rules than their integrated competitors.[21] Most mini-mills have located in scrap-abundant areas that enjoy natural protection from integrated producers by virtue of transport costs. Most have concentrated on simple, low-value-added products such as wire rod and reinforcing bar that need not be produced to high metallurgical standards, leaving to integrated producers the flat-rolled sheet used in automobiles and appliances. Most have enjoyed, in contrast to their integrated brethren, financial success through the late 1970s and early 1980s. Currently mini-mills account for roughly 20 percent of domestic steel shipments (Table 2.4).

Increasingly, the technologies utilized by mini-mills and large integrated plants show a tendency to converge, although some such as Hogan (1987) question whether mini-mills will encroach significantly on product lines dominated by integrated firms. In January 1987, Nucor, one of the leaders of the mini-mill segment of the industry, announced plans to construct a state-of-the-art steel complex, slated for completion in 1989. Production will be based on a new technology that permits high-quality steel to be produced on a mini-mill scale, enabling that segment of the industry to produce flat-rolled steel products. The critical technological breakthrough is a caster developed by a West German firm. The new machine employs a funnel-shaped mold (called a "tunnel furnace") which permits strip coming off the new caster to be passed directly to the strip mill, eliminating the need for slab reheating furnaces and a roughing mill and achieving a saving of capital and operating costs of at least 50 percent.[22] Since the furnace and mill are adjoining, the hot strip mill should receive slabs at a consistent temperature, facilitating the production of more consistent and higher quality steel.

Integrated producers have responded with new techniques of their own. To protect their market among the automakers, in the first half of 1986 they opened five new electrogalvanizing lines designed to provide the automobile industry with corrosion resistant, uniformly formable steel. Chrysler, for example, plans to convert most of its exterior panels from hot-dip galvanized to electrogalvanized steel during the 1988 model year.[23]

Another innovation is plasma steelmaking, which produces molten steel directly from iron ore, taking advantage of the heat intensity and chemical activity of which plasma is capable. Traditionally, the production of high purity steel requires the combination of blast furnace smelting, hot metal pretreatment, basic oxygen furnace refining and secondary refining. In contrast, plasma steelmaking produces clean steel with low phosphorus and sulfur content in a single process, in which iron ore is reduced in a plasma-state reducing gas. Metal is injected into a plasma stream of high temperature and then is melted and sprayed onto another material, imparting to it corrosion and heat resistance. The method is presently used in the production of components for jet engines, satellites and computers.

In textiles, large investments have been made in open-end spinning, automatic chute feeders, and automatic doffers. Open-end spinning increases spinning speed by at least 350 percent, eliminates the roving and winding processes (reducing the number of steps involved in manufacturing some types of yarn from 15 to 3), and offers improved yarn quality and uniformity. The spread of the shuttleless loom also has accelerated in recent years. Not only do they operate at three times the speed of traditional looms, but shuttleless looms can produce seven to eight times the fabric because they weave wider widths. They are also safer and quieter, better satisfying OSHA regulations (which may have provided additional impetus for modernization by the U.S. industry). On the other hand, they are less versatile than ring spindles, which permit the direction of twisting to be freely changed and can utilize woollen and worsted as well as dry flax materials. In 1984 one third of weaving machines in operation in the U.S. were shuttleless.[24]

Textile finishing has benefited from accelerating printing speeds as a result of improvements in automatic rotary screen printing. New machines are able to print a wider variety of color combinations. Automatic control and computer systems have been applied to dyeing, patterning and other finishing operations, reducing labor costs and improving quality.

In apparel, where the vast majority of value added continues to derive from painstakingly labor-intensive processes, technological progress has proceeded more slowly. Ninety percent of value added in clothing is formed by sewing, which remains essentially a batch process with much manual time devoted to material handling. Although sewing machine speeds have been increased by 50 percent over the last two decades, machine operation accounts for under a quarter of an operative's time.[25] Advances with more scope for reducing labor costs include work-space management systems and technology such as laser cutting and computer-assisted pocket setting and stitching systems. Computer-aided garment design is increasingly prevalent. Manufacturers are also enthusiastic about the potential offered by computer-based marketing systems. Terminals already link retail outlets directly with textile mills and apparel manufacturers, cutting time between order and delivery and reducing inventory carrying costs.

The automakers continue to pursue both process and product innovations. Process innovations include efforts to reduce the number of stamping operations required per part. The cost of shaping and assembling a car frame is fully $400 lower in Japan than in the United States due both to the greater thickness of body panels on U.S. cars and to their more complicated design. Body panels on Japanese cars are typically 3 to 4 inches thick and must be stamped 4 or 5 times to be formed. U.S. outer panels are typically 5 to 8 inches thick and require 8 or more presses. Increasingly, U.S. automakers are paying attention to the process-driven design in their attempt to reduce stamping and assembly costs.[26]

Three representative product innovations are the antilock brake, GM's Quad 4 engine and the continuously variable transmission. As part of the antilock braking system, a microprocessor under the dash is linked to sensors in each wheel. When the brakes lock, the computer automatically pumps the brakes, up to 14 times a second, so that the wheels retain traction and stop the car in a straight line. For two years this system has been standard on most BMW and Mercedes models and on Ford's luxury line. As an option, antilock brakes add from $900 to $1500 to the retail price of the vehicle.[27]

The continuously variable transmission (CVT) is actually a new variant of a technology utilized in Europe as early as 1955. It dispenses with the gearing steps used in automatic transmissions, substituting a metal belt connecting two pulleys, one attached to the engine, the other to the drive shaft. The pulleys achieve the same effects as gears by changing their size. This device promises to reduce fuel consumption by as much as 15 percent by permitting the engine to operate within its most efficient range and offers more rapid acceleration than conventional transmissions. Unlike the CVTs sold in Europe by DAF, those utilized by Ford, Fiat and Subaru employ metal rather than rubber belts. Currently, the technology is feasible only for use on subcompacts; the problem for automakers is how to build CVT transmissions hefty enough for use on larger cars.[28]

The Quad 4 engine developed by GM uses computer technology to increase the power output of the four cylinder engine.[29] Dispensing with the distributor and spark plug wires, its dedicated computer triggers a small electrical coil atop each plug, calculating the timing using data transmitted from a sensor on the crankshaft. The individual coils permit precise firing, high voltages and hence greater-than-conventional power out. GM has built a Quad 4 plant near Lansing, Michigan scheduled to produce 1,000 of the engines daily by the beginning of 1988. At the time of writing the engine will be available in 1988 as an option on three of GM's larger cars.

Joint Ventures and Migrant Firms

The prevalence of joint ventures with foreign corporations and of production on American soil by foreign basic-industry firms has increased significantly in recent years. Through joint ventures, U.S. firms acquire knowledge of foreign technologies and labor-management techniques; through joint ventures and solely-owned subsidiaries, their foreign counterparts gain a U.S. presence as a hedge against currency fluctuations and protectionist threats.

The trend has been most visible in the automobile industry. Mazda recently joined Honda, Nissan and Toyota in producing cars in the United States. Toyota's highly successful joint venture with GM in Fremont, California was analyzed above. Another Toyota plant is scheduled to commence production in 1988, while two more Japanese plants and a Chrysler-Mitsubishi joint venture are in the development stage in the U.S., with four Japanese and South Korean plants planned or under construction in Canada. Ford and Nissan are exploring the possibility of joint production at Ford's Avon Lake, Ohio plant. By 1990, according to industry estimates, these plants will have a combined capacity of more than 2 million units.[30]

In textiles, the predominant form of joint venture is foreign production by U.S. manufacturers. Joint ventures (as well as manufacturer-owned plants abroad) are seen as an alternative to the traditional practice of subcontracting production to foreign firms as a way of capitalizing on lower foreign labor costs. The advantages of joint ventures and wholly-owned subsidiaries accrue in the form of enhanced quality control. The practice is utilized for unskilled and semi-skilled labor-intensive operations as carried out by U.S. corporate subsidiaries operating in Mexico, for example. So far, this practice is largely limited to nontraditional firms such as Calvin Klein, Ralph Lauren and other brand names. The share of their product mix accounted for by imports is expected to reach 35 percent by the mid-1990s.

Over the last four years, a number of Japanese steel producers have acquired stakes in the U.S. integrated steel sector. Recently, they have been joined by the Koreans. A U.S. steel mill in Pittsburg, California is now partially owned by the Korean-backed USS-Posco Industries. The rebuilt plant will utilize technology from Pohang Iron and Steel Company Ltd., the Korean corporation that has jointly owned the plant with USX since April 1986. In addition, foreign owners have held a controlling interest in at least ten U.S.-based mini-mills. Many of these investments promise to pay handsomely now that U.S. production costs have fallen relative to those in Japan. Yet as of 1987 only half a dozen mini-mills remained under the control of foreign interests. In a number of cases foreign owners had difficulty in exporting offshore management styles to the U.S. In others it is argued that they simply paid too little attention to their relatively modest American holdings.[31]

EVALUATING THE EFFECTS OF U.S. FISCAL POLICY

The previous section identified a number of factors that have influenced the performance of the basic industries in this decade. In this section, we attempt to assess the significance of one of these factors: U.S. fiscal policy. To do this, we employ a computable general equilibrium (CGE) model that captures the responses of U.S. industries to changes in government policy and other economic conditions. We begin with a brief description of the structure of the model; further details may be found in Goulder and

Eichengreen (1988). We then report simulation experiments designed to isolate the effects of changes in government spending and taxes since 1980.

The model distinguishes ten U.S. sectors: agriculture and mining, crude petroleum and refining, construction, the textile and apparel complex, metals, machinery, motor vehicles, miscellaneous manufacturing, services and housing. This disaggregation permits usto address a number of issues central to the current debate over U.S. competitiveness: the effects of restrictions on agricultural trade; of import penetration in textiles, steel and automobiles; and of increased trade in services. Goods produced by each of these industries are treated as imperfect substitutes for goods produced by their foreign competitors; hence changes in the relative prices of domestic and foreign goods lead to shifts in demand.

Firms combine the cost-minimizing levels of labor and intermediate inputs with the existing capital stock to produce output. Industry capital stocks change from year to year as a result of firms' investment decisions. Intermediate inputs can be obtained both at home and abroad, and firms seeking to minimize costs alter the mix of domestic and imported intermediates utilized when relative prices change. Intersectoral transactions are tracked through the use of a U.S. input-output table.

Managers pursue investment strategies aimed at maximizing the value of the firm (equivalently, the present value of after-tax dividends less the present value of new equity issues). In making investment decisions, managers are concerned not just with current profitability but with expected future profits as well; hence they must formulate forecasts of the future. To insure that they adopt intelligent (and model-consistent) forecasts, we impose the rational-expectations assumption. Because rapid investment is costly (reflecting not just costs of purchasing equipment but of disrupting production while new equipment is installed), it proceeds gradually until the new desired capital intensity is achieved. The explicit treatment of forward-looking investment decisions distinguishes this model from other CGE models.

Households also behave in a sophisticated forward-looking fashion. Their objective is to choose paths of consumption and of financial holdings that maximize utility. Utility is a function of consumption now and in the future, and is maximized subject to an intertemporal budget constraint. Financial wealth is the means of carrying over purchasing power from year to year. If, for example, households anticipate that their income will rise in the future, they increase their consumption now, since they wish to smooth the profile of consumption over time; to do so they run down their savings or borrow now and repay in the future out of their then higher incomes, respecting the intertemporal budget constraint. A distinguishing feature of our model is that liabilities of firms and assets of households are treated in a consistent fashion. If firms issue debt or equity to finance investment, that same debt or equity must be willingly held by households. The accounting identity linking the corporate and household sectors is an explicit feature of our model.

Overall consumption by households is divided into 17 individual categories of consumption goods produced by our ten industries. Households first decide on the shares of those 17 categories in their total consumption (as a function of relative prices); they then divide their spending within categories between domestic and imported goods (again, as a function of relative prices). Households face a similar allocation problem on the financial side: they must choose the shares of their portfolios allocated to assets issued by domestic and foreign firms. They are assumed to shift the composition of their portfolios toward assets offering relatively high rates of return but to resist placing too much of their wealth in any one asset because of the risk this implies. Interest rates and stock prices adjust so that the existing stock of assets is willingly held.

The government sector in the model has three functions: collecting taxes, distributing transfers, and purchasing goods and services. Transfers and purchases are specified as fixed shares of overall spending, with purchases allocated to specific producer goods according to fixed expenditure shares. The model specifies each of the major taxes in the United States and provides special detail on provisions of the tax code likely to influence investment, such as profits taxes, investment tax credits and capital gains taxes. Like households, the government faces an intertemporal budget constraint. If the government runs a deficit in a given year, it must pay interest on the additional debt so long as it remains outstanding. In the long run the government is obliged to bring in sufficient tax revenues (relative to spending) to restore the debt-GNP to "traditional" levels.

Along with this detailed treatment of the domestic economy, there is a simpler treatment of the foreign economy. Foreign industry produces the same types of goods as does domestic industry. Changes in foreign production costs are reflected in the prices of foreign goods. The foreign government performs the same functions and has the same tax instruments as the domestic government. Foreign consumers demand the same goods as U.S. consumers, their utility-maximizing behavior serving as the source of foreign demand for U.S. exports. Like domestic households, foreign households divide their portfolios into shares comprised of claims on U.S. firms and claims on firms in their countries of residence. Investors are assumed to display "home-country preference"; that is, foreigners prefer to hold most of their wealth in the form of non-dollar assets, while U.S. residents hold most of their wealth in dollars.

A distinguishing feature of our model is its treatment of the balance of payments. Previous CGE models which recognize the existence of international transactions focus exclusively on the balance of trade. In contrast, our model provides an integrated treatment of the current and capital accounts of the balance of payments. The current account equals the trade balance (the difference between exports and imports) plus the flow of interest payments on the (endogenously determined) value of U.S. foreign investments net of payments to foreign owners of U.S. assets. The capital account of the balance of payments is derived from the flow demands of domestic residents for additional foreign assets for their portfolios, net of sales of domestic assets demanded by foreign residents for addition to their portfolios. The current and capital accounts must sum to zero by the balance of payments identity; the exchange rate, interest rates, and prices adjust to insure that this identity is respected. As the experience of recent years has revealed the effects of government policies can be very different depending on the degree of international capital mobility; our model permits those effects to be estimated under different assumptions about the responsiveness of capital flows.

With its attention to adjustment dynamics, the model is capable of contrasting the short- and long-run effects of changes in economic conditions. Short- and long-run responses differ because firms adjust their capital stocks gradually over time in response to changes in the incentive to invest, while households accumulate or dispose of assets gradually in response to changes in the incentive to save. Many recent debates about the relationship of exchange rates to international competitiveness focus on issues of dynamics; a prominent example is whether the trade balance follows a J curve in response to exchange-rate depreciation, worsening initially but strengthening subsequently. With its explicit treatment of the dynamics of adjustment in both corporate and household sectors, our model is capable of addressing such questions.

Simulation Results

Beginning in 1981, the U.S. government introduced several significant changes in fiscal policy. Table 2.5 displays Federal spending, receipts, and budget deficits over the period 1980-1986. In 1980, total Federal expenditure (government purchases, transfers, and interest payments) was approximately 22.5 percent of GNP. Since that time, Federal expenditure has increased as a percentage of GNP, reaching 24.7 percent in 1982 and subsequently remaining above 23.8 percent.[32] On the tax side, the Economic Recovery Tax Act of 1981 (ERTA) and the Tax Equity and Fiscal Responsibility Act of 1982 (TEFRA) introduced important changes in effective tax rates. Important provisions of these measures included the implementation of accelerated depreciation provisions (by reducing the tax lives of depreciable assets) and the reduction in marginal tax rates on individual incomes. From Table 2.5 it is clear that these changes were followed by a decline in tax revenues as a percentage of GNP), although the specific contribution of tax revisions to the observed changes in revenues remains a matter of some debate. During the period 1980-1986, the fraction of GNP represented by Federal receipts fell from 20.3 to 19.6 percent. Together, the increases in spending and the reductions in revenues (relative to GNP) produced the substantial increases in Federal budget deficits that have gained such notoriety in recent years.

How did these changes affect the basic industries? To answer this question, we simulate the U.S. economy under two general sets of conditions. In the first, or base case, simulation, we consider a scenario with no post-1980 changes in fiscal policy, and all tax rates and spending shares at 1980 levels. In the second, or revised case, simulation, we implement the historical changes in U.S. fiscal policy by setting Federal spending shares equal to the values given in Table 2.5 and altering statutory tax rates (effective rates of tax depreciation and marginal tax rates on individual income) to conform to the 1981-82 ERTA and TEFRA revisions.[33] By comparing the base and revised cases, we are able to isolate the influence exorted by the changes in fiscal policy of the early 1980s.

Table 2.5

Federal Expenditures, Receipts, and Deficits, 1980-86*

Year	GNP	Expenditures	Receipts	Deficit
1980	2732.0	615.1 (22.51)	553.8 (20.27)	61.3 (2.24)
1981	3052.6	703.3 (23.04)	639.5 (20.95)	63.8 (2.09)
1982	3166.0	781.2 (24.67)	635.3 (20.07)	145.9 (4.61)
1983	3405.7	835.9 (24.54)	659.9 (19.38)	176.0 (5.17)
1984	3765.0	896.5 (23.81)	726.5 (19.30)	170.0 (4.52)
1985	3998.1	984.9 (24.63)	786.8 (19.68)	198.0 (4.95)
1986	4208.5	1030.2 (24.48)	826.2 (19.63)	204.0 (4.85)

*All values are in billions of current dollars. Figures in parentheses express the values as percentages of GNP. Source of all data is Economic Report of the President, January 1987. (thus, these experiments do not incorporate the Tax Reform Act of 1886 or potential future tax policy changes).

Since the behavior of producers and households is forward-looking, to perform simulations we need to specify future as well as current fiscal policies. In the base case simulation, 1980 tax rates and spending shares are assumed to continue to prevail indefinitely. In revised case simulations, we assume on the tax side that there are no further changes in tax rates after 1986 (thus, these experiments do not incorporate the Tax Reform Act of 1986 or potential future tax policy changes); we assume on the spending side that Federal spending's share of GNP is gradually reduced to its 1980 value (22.51 percent). The revised case simulations actually distinguish three scenarios that differ in the number of years assumed to be required to reduce the government spending share of GNP to 1980 levels. The "fast", "moderate," and "slow" spending-reduction scenarios assume that the government spending share is restored to its 1980 value by 1990, 1992, and 1996, respectively.

Results appear in Tables 2.6-2.9. Table 2.6 summarizes the effects of the fiscal initiatives on the macroeconomy. Whatever the assumption about future spending reductions, the fiscal expansion implies relatively small increases in the value of the dollar (as measured by the changes in the nominal exchange rate) -- much smaller than the increase that occurred over the period 1980-1985. The implication -- that much of the explanation for the rise and fall of the dollar since 1980 lies beyond the realm of U.S. tax and spending policies narrowly defined -- is similarly the conclusion of most other studies of recent exchange rate fluctuations. As noted above, there is no shortage of supplementary explanations: the shift toward tight monetary policy that accompanied fiscal expansion in the United States, tight fiscal policies in other OECD countries, safe haven demands for dollar-denominated assets, and the possibility of a speculative bubble. What is striking about our results is how little of the dollar's post-1980 rise and fall is replicated in simulations which incorporate only the changes in domestic fiscal policy. It is important to interpret these results cautiously, since many of the specific features of our model work to minimize the aggregate effects of fiscal policy. We assume assume throughout that markets clear in both the short and long run and that investors accurately anticipate the higher taxes or lower spending levels that ultimately will be required to balance the budget. Appending wage and price rigidities that interfere with continuous market clearing or positing that consumers and producers act myopically would tend to magnify the effects of fiscal policies.

Since our fiscal policy simulations replicate only a small share of the observed rise and fall of the dollar, it is not surprising that they account for only a portion of historical movements in other macroeconomic variables. Importantly, however, all of the simulated variables move in directions consistent with their actual behavior.

Table 2.6 summarizes the effects of the fiscal expansion on consumption, investment, exports and imports. Over most of the '80s, budget deficits absorb a significant portion of domestic saving and crowd out aggregate investment; in the 1990s, as spending and deficits are reduced to "normal" levels, investment recovers, however. In the long run, investment actually rises above base case levels (the levels that would have occurred if there had been no change in fiscal policy), reflecting the supply-side orientation of the 1981-1982 changes in tax policy. (Both the accelerated depreciation provisions and the reductions in marginal tax rates promote higher saving and investment.) But in the short run, these stimuli are more than offset by the crowding-out effects of higher Federal spending.

In keeping with the modest effects on the exchange rate, the effects on import and export values (and quantities) are relatively small. In the short run, the rise in the dollar depresses exports and stimulates imports. Although many observers claim that U.S. budget deficits are at the heart of the trade deficit problem, these results imply that the deficits themselves played at most a supporting role.

Table 2.7 highlights the impact of the fiscal policy changes on specific industries. These impacts differ substantially. While profits, employment, and output fall in the short run in a number of industries, in the construction, metals, and machinery industries, each of these variables rises (relative to the base case). These increases stem from the fact that a very large share of incremental government spending is devoted to purchases of goods from these three industries, as indicated by Table 2.8.

Table 2.7 also reveals significant differences across industries in effects on investment. Although aggregate private investment falls (as indicated in Table 2.6) in the short run, in a majority of industries investment rises (relative to the base case). The negative effects on investment are largest in the housing services industry. This is the case for three reasons. First, the performance of this industry is highly sensitive to interest rate changes, since

Table 2.6

Implications of Fiscal Policy Changes for Aggregate Economic Variables
(percentage changes from base case)

Scenario:*	Exchange Rate			Consumption			Investment			Exports			Imports		
	F	M	S	F	M	S	F	M	S	F	M	S	F	M	S
YEAR															
1981	0.58	0.59	0.65	-2.65	-2.69	-2.62	-3.54	-3.51	-3.63	-0.09	-0.09	-0.16	0.37	0.37	0.35
1982	2.51	2.48	2.54	-3.50	-3.52	-3.46	-2.17	-2.16	-2.23	-1.97	-1.94	-2.01	0.68	0.67	0.70
1983	1.91	1.88	1.92	-3.05	-3.08	-3.03	-2.24	-2.23	-2.33	-1.49	-1.45	-1.50	0.37	0.36	0.38
1984	1.11	1.08	1.10	-2.44	-2.48	-2.44	-2.04	-2.04	-2.16	-0.83	-0.79	-0.82	0.03	0.01	0.01
1985	0.33	0.32	0.30	-1.77	-1.82	-1.81	-1.63	-1.66	-1.81	-0.19	-0.16	-0.16	-0.27	-0.29	-0.30
1986	-0.67	-0.65	-0.68	-0.92	-1.00	-1.02	-2.13	-2.21	-2.43	0.70	0.70	0.71	-0.76	-0.77	-0.80
1987	-1.21	-1.11	-1.12	-0.32	-0.44	-0.52	-1.49	-1.65	-1.96	1.10	1.03	1.03	-0.90	-0.90	-0.93
1988	-1.70	-1.44	-1.36	0.28	0.07	-0.09	-0.71	-1.05	-1.50	1.50	1.26	1.18	-1.00	-0.95	-0.97
1989	-2.34	-1.70	-1.39	0.95	0.56	0.25	0.29	-0.37	-1.11	2.08	1.48	1.17	-1.12	-0.97	-0.93
1990	-2.47	-1.83	-1.37	1.39	0.99	0.55	1.04	0.28	-1.70	2.23	1.60	1.12	-1.07	-0.93	-0.86
1995	0.10	-0.11	0.74	1.57	1.63	1.63	2.14	2.03	1.39	0.21	0.33	0.70	0.14	0.02	0.32
2000	1.40	1.32	0.87	1.57	1.62	1.67	2.93	2.86	2.44	-0.55	-0.54	-0.34	0.80	0.75	0.51
2010	2.26	2.24	2.26	1.45	1.48	1.52	3.82	3.78	3.62	-0.66	-0.67	-0.82	1.30	1.28	1.27

*Scenarios F, M, and S denote fast, moderate, and slow spending reduction cases, respectively. See text for details.

Table 2.7
Effects across Industries of U.S. Fiscal Policy Changes
(percentage changes from base case)

Industry:	(1) Agriculture and Mining			(2) Crude Petroleum and Refining			(3) Construction			(4) Textiles, Apparel and Leather			(5) Metals		
Year:	1982	1990	2000	1982	1990	2000	1982	1990	2000	1982	1990	2000	1982	1990	2000

HISTORICAL SPENDING AND TAX CHANGES

(1) Fast Spending Reduction

Investment	-1.16	3.27	3.92	0.88	5.57	6.84	-2.46	-0.07	3.40	0.46	5.81	7.96	1.46	3.00	6.60
Profits	-0.29	2.09	-0.90	-2.33	7.84	5.96	2.42	-1.78	3.02	-5.66	7.94	7.08	6.51	1.47	4.69
Employment	-0.64	0.68	-2.50	-2.30	2.43	-1.13	1.93	-1.36	1.05	-4.51	2.84	0.84	6.97	-3.58	-1.90
Output	-0.36	0.57	1.18	-1.15	1.20	2.06	1.83	-1.43	1.06	-3.97	2.56	1.39	5.63	-2.96	-1.03

(2) Moderate Spending Reduction

Investment	1.26	2.52	3.87	0.94	4.48	6.80	-2.38	-1.12	3.26	0.49	4.83	7.92	1.64	1.99	6.42
Profits	-0.26	1.43	-0.84	-2.31	6.50	5.97	2.43	-1.73	2.82	-5.65	5.56	7.11	6.55	1.28	4.40
Employment	-0.62	0.31	-2.40	-2.28	1.83	-1.03	1.93	-1.24	-0.93	-4.51	2.12	0.94	7.00	-2.52	-2.09
Output	-0.36	0.48	1.15	-1.14	0.94	2.00	1.83	-1.32	0.92	-3.97	1.93	1.46	5.66	-2.07	-1.22

(3) Slow Spending Reduction

Investment	1.18	1.81	3.89	0.69	2.83	6.46	-2.58	-2.43	2.53	0.40	3.56	7.60	1.47	0.72	5.67
Profits	-0.29	1.19	-0.70	-2.35	6.14	6.16	2.37	-1.72	2.07	-5.65	4.98	7.21	6.47	2.46	3.67
Employment	-0.64	0.03	-2.13	-2.31	1.42	-0.53	1.88	-1.26	0.46	-4.50	1.46	1.26	6.93	-1.40	-2.47
Output	-0.37	0.38	1.05	-1.18	0.62	1.74	1.78	-1.34	0.42	-3.96	1.34	1.66	5.60	-1.16	-1.69

Table 2.7 (cont.)

Effects Across Industries of U.S. Fiscal Policy Changes
(percentage changes from base case)

Industry:	(1) Agriculture and Mining			(2) Crude Petroleum and Refining			(3) Construction			(4) Textiles, Apparel and Leather			(5) Metals		
Period:	1982	1990	2000	1982	1990	2000	1982	1990	2000	1982	1990	2000	1982	1990	2000

HISTORICAL SPENDING CHANGES, NO TAX CHANGES

(4) Moderate Spending Reduction

Investment	-3.31	-1.25	-0.28	-6.40	-1.81	-0.38	-4.97	-4.34	-1.44	-5.57	-1.93	-0.48	-4.19	-4.21	-1.78
Profits	-1.65	1.85	0.43	-2.84	-0.23	0.04	1.04	-3.97	-1.90	-5.32	-1.87	0.27	5.59	-4.89	-2.27
Employment	-1.67	2.59	0.74	-2.65	2.33	0.73	0.57	-2.35	-1.21	-3.94	1.54	0.75	6.29	-1.60	-1.57
Output	-0.37	-0.65	-0.42	-1.01	-0.87	-0.74	0.58	-2.48	-1.29	-3.41	0.93	0.44	5.20	-1.87	-1.80

Table 2.7 (cont.)

Effects across Industries of U.S. Fiscal Policy Changes
(percentage changes from base case)

Industry:	(6) Machinery			(7) Motor Vehicles			(8) Misc. Manufacturing			(9) Services			(10) Housing		
Year:	1982	1990	2000	1982	1990	2000	1982	1990	2000	1982	1990	2000	1982	1990	2000

HISTORICAL SPENDING AND TAX CHANGES

(1) Fast Spending Reduction

Investment	1.09	1.25	4.73	-1.53	3.66	6.02	1.28	5.13	7.87	0.43	4.98	7.96	-5.21	-2.83	-1.74
Profits	9.22	-0.42	3.36	-2.88	4.79	5.47	-0.23	3.96	6.53	-1.78	5.32	7.04	-9.81	2.02	2.92
Employment	8.64	-4.50	-2.17	-3.39	2.26	0.80	-0.29	0.23	0.08	-1.19	0.59	0.28	-7.26	2.83	1.84
Output	6.91	-3.82	-1.44	-2.69	1.59	1.44	-0.34	0.31	1.01	-1.02	0.48	1.03	1.76	-2.99	-2.63

(2) Moderate Spending Reduction

Investment	1.32	0.28	4.55	-1.51	2.63	5.96	1.34	4.10	7.79	0.48	3.94	7.88	-5.25	-3.30	-1.79
Profits	9.27	-0.07	3.05	-2.88	3.67	5.44	-0.22	3.21	6.45	-1.77	3.67	6.96	-9.85	-0.22	3.05
Employment	8.67	-3.11	-2.38	-3.39	1.63	0.88	-0.29	0.17	0.08	-1.19	0.44	0.31	-7.30	2.05	2.03
Output	6.93	-2.65	-1.66	-2.69	1.09	1.46	-0.34	0.26	0.97	-1.03	0.37	1.02	1.77	-2.94	-2.78

(3) Slow Spending Reduction

Investment	1.17	-0.83	3.78	-1.66	1.27	5.56	1.12	2.75	7.24	0.40	2.64	7.41	-5.29	-3.96	-2.17
Profits	9.20	1.63	2.32	-2.89	3.13	5.29	-0.24	3.20	6.20	-1.76	3.61	6.65	-9.81	-1.01	3.26
Employment	8.62	-1.64	-2.81	-3.40	1.00	1.10	-0.30	0.13	0.13	-1.17	0.28	0.39	-7.26	1.18	2.45
Output	6.89	-1.44	-2.18	-2.69	0.57	1.47	-0.35	0.20	0.85	-1.02	0.23	0.94	1.79	-2.85	-3.19

Table 2.7 (cont.)

Effects across Industries of U.S. Fiscal Policy Changes
(percentage changes from base case)

Industry:	(6) Machinery			(7) Motor Vehicles			(8) Misc. Manufacturing			(9) Services			(10) Housing		
Year:	1982	1990	2000	1982	1990	2000	1982	1990	2000	1982	1990	2000	1982	1990	2000

HISTORICAL SPENDING
CHANGES, NO TAX CHANGES

(4) Moderate Spending Reduction

Investment	-5.80	-4.38	-1.81	-2.51	-0.59	-5.26	-2.89	-0.81	-5.63	-2.81	-0.84	-3.32	-1.96	-0.81	
Profits	-3.22	-4.86	-2.30	-1.74	-0.33	-0.43	-2.45	-0.59	-1.82	-3.66	-0.54	-6.52	-1.13	1.27	
Employment	-3.59	-1.85	-1.71	1.06	0.59	-0.31	0.08	0.03	-0.93	0.33	0.33	-5.27	1.86	1.81	
Output	-2.71	-2.07	-1.95	-0.04	0.04	-0.20	-0.59	-0.39	-0.68	-0.34	-0.18	1.15	-2.00	-1.61	

Table 2.8

Shares of Government Purchases Devoted to Different Industries

Industry	Expenditure Share
1. Agriculture and Mining	.0023
2. Crude Petroleum and Refining	.0186
3. Construction	.1436
4. Textiles, Apparel, and Leather	.0029
5. Metals	.2684
6. Machinery	.2491
7. Motor Vehicles	.0075
8. Misc. Manufacturing	.1163
9. Services	.1811
10. Housing	.0102

the debt-equity ratio in this industry is especially high and a large fraction of investment is new housing capital is financed by debt. As a result, the increase in interest rates occasioned by higher budget deficits particularly hurts the housing industry. Second, the 1981 and 1982 cuts in individual income tax rates hurt housing in relation to other industries. The imputed rental income to owner-occupied housing is not subject to individual income tax; thus, the tax cuts mainly increase the attractiveness of owning non-housing assets by lowering the tax on the capital income that they generate. Finally, the changes in depreciation rules over the period 1981-85 apply mainly to incorporated industries; since only a small fraction (less than three percent) of housing is corporation-owned, these changes principally benefit non-housing industries.

The reduced overall rate of investment helps explain the cutback in investment by the construction industry, since this industry supplies a large proportion of new capital. Investment rises substantially in the metals and machinery industries, in part reflecting the fact that large shares of the increase in government spending are devoted to these industries.

These results indicate that, in the short run, changes in U.S. fiscal policy during the first half of this decade generally had adverse effects on the basic industries. While the steel industry seems to have benefited, the textile and apparel complex and the auto industry were not helped.

The long-term implications of these fiscal revisions differ dramatically from their short-term effects. Consider, for example, the results in Table 2.9 for the year 2000 under the moderate spending reduction scenario. While output falls in the short run in most industries, in the long term it rises (relative to the base case) in all industries except metals, machinery, and housing services. The metals and machinery industries, which experienced boosts in output in the short run, have lower output in the long run. These differences reflect the components of fiscal policy that dominate industry performance in the short and long run. In the short run, in industries other than housing the changes in industry performance are dominated by the allocation of government spending. In the long run, government spending returns to its "normal" relationship to GNP, and only the tax side of fiscal policy differs from the base case. The changes in depreciation rules, in particular, are significant in the long run. The petroleum and refining industry, which enjoys the most favorable changes in depreciation rules, exhibits the largest long-term increase in output. In the metals and machinery industries, the changes in depreciation rules are modest, and long-run output falls.

Table 2.9

Aggregate Effects of Historical and Counterfactual Fiscal Policy Changes
(percentage changes from base case)

Scenario:*	Exchange Rate		Consumption		Investment		Exports		Imports	
	M	M'	M	M'	M	M'	M	M'	M	M'
YEAR										
1981	0.59	1.56	-2.69	-1.90	-3.51	-3.00	-0.09	-1.16	0.37	0.21
1982	2.48	2.90	-3.52	-2.53	-2.16	-4.34	-1.94	-2.46	0.67	0.63
1983	1.88	2.35	-3.08	-2.41	-2.23	-4.59	-1.45	-2.16	0.36	0.34
1984	1.08	1.56	-2.48	-2.14	-2.04	-4.61	-0.79	-1.65	0.01	-0.02
1985	0.32	0.81	-1.82	-1.66	-4.51	-0.16	-1.29	-0.29	-0.35	-0.22
1986	-0.65	-0.13	-1.00	-1.38	-2.21	-4.15	0.70	-0.48	-0.77	-0.71
1987	-1.11	-0.81	-0.44	-0.99	-1.65	-3.79	1.03	0.01	-0.90	-0.95
1988	-1.44	-1.39	0.07	-0.61	-1.05	-3.37	1.26	0.43	-0.95	-1.13
1989	-1.70	-1.93	0.56	-0.22	-0.37	-2.86	1.48	0.85	-0.97	-1.29
1990	-1.83	-2.32	0.99	0.13	0.28	-2.36	1.60	1.17	-0.93	-1.37
1995	-0.11	-1.51	1.63	0.50	2.03	-1.20	0.33	0.49	0.02	-0.85
2000	1.32	-0.57	1.62	0.38	2.86	-0.82	-0.54	-0.19	0.75	-0.38
2010	2.24	0.00	1.48	0.20	3.78	-0.39	-0.67	-0.09	1.28	-0.06

*Scenario M incorporates historical spending and tax changes. Scenario M' incorporates historical spending but no tax changes. See text for details.

In the long-run, investment (as opposed to output) rises in all industries except housing. The long-run increases in investment reflect the incentives associated with lower marginal tax rates and accelerated depreciation and parallel the aggregate investment results discussed previously. The long-run decline in housing investment is explained by the same tax features as those mentioned in the context of the short-term decline in housing investment: the exclusion of imputed housing rentals from the individual income tax, and the irrelevance to housing of the 1982-85 changes in depreciation rules.

In assessing these results -- especially the long-term impacts -- it is important to keep in mind that our experiments do not capture the effects of the Tax Reform Act of 1986. To assess the overall long-term consequences of all fiscal policy changes since 1980, one would need to perform simulations that incorporate not only the 1981-86 changes but also the effects of the new tax law. While this is beyond the scope of the present paper, a simulation study by Goulder and Summers (1987) indicates that the 1986 legislation is likely to have detrimental long-term consequences for investment, profit levels, and output in most industries. This suggests that the long-term effects shown in Tables 2.6 and 2.9 may be more favorable than what would emerge once the 1986 tax legislation is taken into account.

As indicated above, the effects of the post-1980 changes in fiscal policy can be decomposed into those stemming from tax and spending changes. To separate out these effects, we perform an additional simulation which incorporates only the changes in government spending. Table 2.9 compares the aggregate effects of this counterfactual experiment with the effects from a simulation in which both tax and spending changes are included. The differences are relatively small in the short term but quite large in the longer term, reinforcing the idea that the changes in tax policy introduced in 1981 and 1982 have their most pronounced effects in the long run. Similar conclusions emerge for particular industries. The last (fourth) set of rows in Table 2.7 contains results from this counterfactual, spending-changes-only simulation. The spending changes in this simulation are the same as those in second (moderate spending reduction) historical simulation. That the results from these simulations are fairly similar in the short term but very different in the long term further substantiates the notion that the tax changes have their most significant effects in the long run.

To test the robustness of these results, we perform additional experiments under alternative assumptions about international capital mobility and behavioral parameters. These experiments indicate that the pattern of results is essentially the same in the absence of international capital mobility and under alternative assumptions about the sensitivity of investment to interest rate changes. Results from these experiments are displayed in the appendix.

Three general conclusions emerge from these simulations. First, the post-1980 changes in U.S. fiscal policy produce small impacts on aggregate economic variables and on specific U.S. industries relative to what has been observed during this decade. Fiscal policy alone cannot explain the magnitude of the swings in the value of the dollar since 1981; nor is it sufficient to account for the significant changes in the performance of the basic industries. Second, in the short term, the most significant effects from fiscal policy stem from changes on the spending side -- in particular, the allocation across industries of the increases in government purchases. Most of the basic industries -- textiles, apparel, leather, motor vehicles -- were adversely affected in the short term, because the reduction in demand from reduced private consumption and investment (crowded out by government spending) was not compensated for by increased government purchases. Only the steel industry enjoyed a net benefit in the short run, since it was the recipient of a disproportionate share of increased government purchases. Finally, the long-term effects of the policy initiatives are very different from their short-term effects, both in the aggregate and at the industry level. Once government spending is restored to its traditional relationship to GNP, this dimension of fiscal policy ceases to have a significant influence on economic performance. The tax side dominates. Our simulation results indicate that tax changes legislated early in this decade will generally favor profits, investment, and output of the U.S. basic industries over the long term.

CONCLUSIONS

In this paper we have provided a broad overview of factors affecting the international competitiveness of U.S. basic industries, followed by a simulation analysis designed to pinpoint the role of U.S. fiscal policy in those industries' changing competitive fortunes. Part one of the paper identified a variety of factors affecting industrial competitiveness, including but not limited to fiscal policy changes. These include changes in the intensity of competition abroad, changes in spending patterns at home, changes in the cost and organization of labor, investment in plant and equipment, and the facility with which basic industry firms develop and implement product and process innovations.

Part two of the paper confirmed that domestic tax and government spending policies provide a part, but only a part, of the explanation for recent swings in the competitive position of the U.S. auto, steel, textile and apparel sectors.

It is noteworthy that only a modest rise and fall of the dollar is generated when we use our model to simulate the effects of U.S. tax and spending policies. A number of factors contribute to this result. First, fiscal policies worked through a number of channels, such as market imperfections and myopic decision rules, not featured in our model. Second, fiscal policies surely interacted with other independent developments contributing to the fluctuation of the dollar, including domestic monetary policies, foreign tax and spending policies, and speculative bubbles in asset markets. Finally, the long-term impact of the 1981-82 tax law revisions is influenced by other subsequent tax reforms -- most notably, the Tax Reform Act of 1986. A full treatment of the effects of fiscal policies in the 1980s will require closer attention to these factors.

Notes

1. For sources of statistics not otherwise cited in this paper, see Eichengreen (1988). The first part of this paper represents an update of that earlier article.

2. The cost of production estimates for steel are by Peter F. Marcus. See "U.S. Steel Mills Could Stage a Major Comeback," Boston Globe, December 22, 1987, p. 48. Similarly, an early 1988 report issued by the U.S. International Trade Commission concluded that the U.S. steel sheet and strip industry is currently one of the most cost competitive among the major industrial countries.

3. National Institute of Economic and Social Research, press release, June 1987.

4. Labor productivity in Figure 3 is product per worker, the ratio of output as measured in Figure 2.1 relative to employment as measured in Figure 2.2.

5. Iron Age, July 4, 1986, p. 13.

6. In addition, in 1986 Ford began exporting the Mercury Tracer from its Hermosillo, Mexico plant.

7. "U.S. Steel Mills Could Stage a Major Comeback," Boston Globe, December 22, 1987, p. 48.

8. In announcing 1987 results, USX announced that $28 million would be paid out in profit sharing on April 15, 1988. 33 Metal Producing (February 1988), p. 15.

9. For details, see Krafcik (1986).

10. Iron Age, March 1987, p. 45; 33 Metal Producing (June 1988), p. 16.

11. San Francisco Chronicle, 31 August 1987; Forbes, September 7, 1987, p. 82.

12. Katz et al. (1987), pp. 2-3.

13. For our purposes, the first measure is more appropriate; while the second conveys information on the amount of "unproductive" labor needed to monitor the production process, it tells us only indirectly about total labor productivity.

14. There is evidence as well that wage concessions are most readily obtained in plants where labor relations are least adversarial and worker participation in decision making is greatest. See Kaufman and Martinez-Vazquez.

15. Precise estimates differ. 5.2 per cent is that of the WEFA Group, a Philadelphia-based consulting firm, cited in New York Times, January 13, 1988.

16. More recently, adjustment against the Taiwan dollar and Korean won has begun, as the three appreciated against the U.S. dollar by 42, 10 and 8 percent, respectively, between January and August 1987.

17. See Krugman (1987) for theoretical analyses of this phenomenon.

18. Ghadar et al. (1987), p. 5.

19. "U.S. and China Agree to Curb Textile Imports," New York Times, December 20, 1987, p. 12.

20. See Barnett and Crandall (1986) for further discussion.

21. Settogan (1987).

22. 33 Metal Producing, February 1987, p. 25. Another estimate put the saving at $75 a ton saving over conventional hot band processing (Iron Age, March 1987, p. 30).

23. Iron Age, July 4, 1986, p. 44.

24. Ghadar, et al. (1987), pp. 74-75.

25. Cable and Baker (1983), pp. 32-33.

26.   Iron Age, April 1987, p. 29.

27.   Forbes, February 9, 1987, p. 116.

28.   Forbes, June 15, 1987, pp. 236-237.

29.   The Quad 4 is only one of several engine advances currently under consideration by U.S. automakers. Also noteworthy is the strateified-charge 2-stroke engine licenced by Ford from Australia. Automotive News (July 4, 1988), p. 1.

30.   Womack (1987), p. 108.

31.   33 Metal Processing, February 1987, pp. 33-36.

32.   The ratio of Federal expenditure to full employment GNP provides a better indicator of the scope of Federal spending. This ratio shows a similar trend since 1981.

33.   The effective rates of tax depreciation were obtained using information from Fullerton and Lyon (1988). Tax rates on individual labor and capital income were obtained from the National Bureau of Economic Research TAXSIM data base.

References

Barnett, Donald and Robert Crandell (1986), Up from the Ashes, Washington, DC: The Brookings Institution.

Cable, Vincent and Betsy Baker (1983), World Textile Trade and Production Trends, London: The Economist.

Cox, W. Michael (1986), "A New Alternative Trade-Weighted Dollar Exchange Rate Index," Economic Review of the Federal Reserve Bank of Dallas (September), pp. 20-28.

Eichengreen, Barry (1988), "International Competition in the Products of U.S. Basic Industries," in Martin Feldstein (ed.), The Changing Role of the United States in the World Economy, Chicago: University of Chicago Press, pp. 279-353.

Feldstein, Martin and Philippe Bachetta (1987), "How Far Has the Dollar Really Fallen?", National Bureau of Economic Research, Working Paper No. 2122.

Frankel, Jeffrey and Kenneth Froot (1987), "The Dollar as a Speculative Bubble: A Tale of Fundamentalists and Chartists," Marcus Wallenberg Papers in International Economics 1, No. 1.

Fullerton, D., and A. Lyon (1988), "Tax Neutrality and Intangible Capital," in L. Summers, ed., Tax Policy and the Economy 2, National Bureau of Economic Research.

General Agreement on Tariffs and Trade (1984), Textiles and Clothing in the World Economy: Appendices I-IV, Geneva: GATT.

Ghadar, Fariborz, William Davidson and Charles Feigenoff (1987), U.S. Industrial Competitiveness: The Case of the Textile and Apparel Industries, Cambridge: Lexington Books.

Goulder, Lawrence and Barry Eichengreen (1987), "Savings Promotion, Investment Promotion and International Competitiveness," in Rob Feenstra (ed.), Exchange Rate and Trade Policies for International Competitiveness, Chicago: University of Chicago Press (forthcoming).

Hogan, William T. (1987), Mini-Mills and Integrated Mills: A Comparison of Steelmaking in the United States, Lexington: Lexington Books.

Hooper, Peter and Catherine Mann (1987), "The U.S. External Deficit: Its Causes and Persistence," paper presented to the Conference on the U.S. Trade Deficit: Causes, Consequences and Cures, Federal Reserve Bank of St. Louis, St. Louis, Mo.

International Textile Manufacturers Federation (1985), 1985 International Production Cost Comparison: Spinning and Weaving, Zurich: ITMF.

Katz, Harry C., Tomas A. Kochan and Jeffrey Keefe (1987), "Industrial Relations and Productivity in the U.S. Automotive Industry," Brookings Papers on Economic Activity, pp. 685-715.

Kaufman, Bruce E. and Jorge Martinez-Vazquez (1988), "Voting for Wage Concessions: The Case of the 1982 GM-UAW Negotiations," Industrial and Labor Relations Review 41, pp. 183-194.

Krafcik, John F. (1986), "Learning from NUMMI," unpublished manuscript, International Motor Vehicle Program, MIT, September 1986.

Krugman, Paul (1987), "Pricing to Market When the Exchange Rate Changes," in Sven Arndt and J. David Richardson, eds., Real-Financial Linkages in Open Economies, Cambridge: MIT Press.

Krugman, Paul and Richard E. Baldwin (1987), "The Persistence of the U.S. Trade Deficit," Brookings Papers in Economic Activity, pp. 1-55.

Mann, Catherine L. (1986), "Prices, Profit Margins and Exchange Rates," Federal Reserve Bulletin 72 (June), pp. 366-379.

Mueller, Hans (1985), "The Changing U.S. Position in the International Steel Market: Output, Trade and Performance," in Milton Hochmuth and William Davidson, eds., Revitalizing American Industry, Cambridge: Ballinger, pp. 213-262.

Womack, James P. (1987), "Prospects for the U.S. Japanese Relationship in the Motor Vehicle Sector," in Cathryn L. Thorp et al., The United States and Mexico: Face to Face with New Technology, Washington, DC: Overseas Development Council.

Appendix

Results from Simulations Performed for Sensitivity Analysis

Table A-1
Aggregate Effects of Fiscal Policy Changes
Under Alternative Parameter Specifications*
(percentage changes from base case)

Year	Exchange Rate				Consumption				Investment			
	M	NK	HI	LI	M	NK	HI	LI	M	NK	HI	LI
1981	0.59	0.81	0.11	0.91	-2.69	-2.77	-2.44	-2.55	-3.51	-3.60	-5.65	-2.92
1982	2.48	0.73	2.22	2.77	-3.52	-3.74	-3.46	-3.36	-2.16	-2.62	-3.00	-2.01
1983	1.88	0.64	1.62	2.17	-3.08	-3.16	-2.99	-2.97	-2.23	-2.58	-3.02	-2.10
1984	1.08	0.48	0.83	1.35	-2.48	-2.45	-2.38	-2.39	-2.04	-2.17	-2.67	-1.99
1985	0.32	0.31	0.06	0.53	-1.82	-1.71	-1.71	-1.76	-1.66	-1.57	-1.95	-1.74
1986	-0.65	0.24	-0.96	-0.48	-1.00	-0.81	-0.84	-0.97	-2.21	-1.86	-3.09	-2.10
1987	-1.11	0.08	-1.36	-1.03	-0.44	-0.24	-0.34	-0.41	-1.65	-1.16	-2.26	-1.70
1988	-1.44	-0.04	-1.61	-1.43	0.07	0.27	0.11	0.10	-1.05	-0.45	-1.35	-1.25
1989	-1.70	-0.13	-1.81	-1.78	0.56	0.75	0.55	0.60	-0.37	0.32	-0.34	-0.74
1990	-1.83	-0.19	-1.89	-1.97	0.99	1.15	0.94	1.02	0.28	1.04	0.63	-0.25
1995	-0.11	0.18	-0.18	-0.36	1.63	1.45	1.56	1.61	2.03	2.57	2.97	1.13
2000	1.32	0.60	1.24	1.14	1.62	1.24	1.57	1.58	2.86	3.16	3.86	1.87
2010	2.24	1.10	2.31	2.36	1.48	1.00	1.45	1.50	3.78	3.99	4.80	2.92

*Scenarios M, NK, HI, and LI denote central case (moderate spending reduction), no international capital mobility, high investment sensitivity, and low investment sensitivity simulations. The investment sensitivity scenarios differ according to the magnitude of adjustment costs associated with installing new capital. The high (low) investment sensitivity case assumes a 50 percent decrease (increase) in the slope of the adjustment cost function relative to the central case. See Goulder and Eichengreen (1988) for details on the specification of this function.

Table A-1 (continued)

Aggregate Effects of Fiscal Policy Changes
Under Alternative Parameter Specifications
(percentage changes from base case)

Year	Exports				Imports			
	M	NK	HI	LI	M	NK	HI	LI
1981	-0.09	-0.30	0.33	-0.39	0.37	-0.30	-0.86	-0.13
1982	-1.94	-0.23	-1.80	-2.20	0.67	-0.23	0.47	0.84
1983	-1.45	-0.27	-1.30	-1.72	0.36	-0.27	0.14	0.54
1984	-0.79	-0.27	-0.66	-1.05	0.01	-0.27	-0.20	0.17
1985	-0.16	-0.25	-0.02	-0.39	-0.29	-0.25	-0.47	-0.15
1986	0.70	-0.29	0.91	0.50	-0.77	0.29	-1.07	-0.63
1987	1.03	-0.25	1.15	0.91	-0.90	-0.25	-1.13	-0.80
1988	1.26	-0.20	1.31	1.22	-0.95	-0.20	-1.12	-0.91
1989	1.48	-0.13	1.47	1.50	-0.97	-0.13	-1.06	-0.98
1990	1.60	-0.05	1.56	1.67	-0.93	-0.05	-0.96	-0.99
1995	0.33	0.24	0.50	0.40	0.02	0.24	0.08	-0.13
2000	-0.54	0.42	-0.26	-0.61	0.75	0.42	0.84	0.59
2010	-0.67	0.67	-0.46	-1.05	1.28	0.67	1.46	1.24

Table A-2
Effects across Industries of Fiscal Policy Changes*
Under Alternative Parameter Specifications
(percentage changes from base case)

Industry:	(1) Agriculture and Mining			(2) Crude Petroleum and Refining			(3) Construction			(4) Textiles, Apparel and Leather			(5) Metals		
Period:	1982	1990	2000	1982	1990	2000	1982	1990	2000	1982	1990	2000	1982	1990	2000
(1) Central Case															
Investment	1.26	2.52	3.87	0.94	4.48	6.80	-2.38	-1.12	3.26	0.49	4.83	7.92	1.64	1.99	6.42
Profits	-0.26	1.43	-0.84	-2.31	6.50	5.97	2.43	-1.73	2.82	-5.65	5.56	7.11	6.55	1.28	4.40
Employ-ment	-0.62	0.31	-2.40	-2.28	1.83	-1.03	1.93	-1.24	0.93	-4.51	2.12	0.94	7.00	-2.52	-2.09
Output	-0.36	0.48	1.15	-1.14	0.94	2.00	1.83	-1.32	0.92	-3.97	1.93	1.46	5.66	-2.07	-1.22
(2) No International Capital Mobility															
Investment	0.46	3.22	4.45	-0.33	5.45	7.81	-3.21	0.08	3.68	-0.14	5.51	8.50	0.68	3.05	7.43
Profits	-0.08	1.25	-1.07	-1.58	5.72	6.73	1.70	-0.81	3.30	-5.79	5.44	7.54	6.06	1.65	5.57
Employ-ment	-0.23	-0.07	-2.67	-1.03	0.64	-0.64	1.41	-0.55	1.21	-3.80	1.42	0.95	7.28	-2.71	-1.35
Output	-0.18	0.31	1.42	-0.71	0.44	2.50	1.35	-0.66	1.23	-3.34	1.32	1.53	5.90	-2.25	-0.49
(3) High Investment Sensitivity															
Investment	2.23	3.09	4.46	1.43	5.40	7.91	-2.64	-0.60	4.49	1.23	6.50	9.71	3.10	2.03	8.17
Profits	-0.10	1.09	-0.90	-2.11	6.67	6.35	1.59	-1.76	3.67	-5.67	5.91	7.70	6.08	1.49	5.39
Employ-ment	-0.38	0.00	-2.69	-1.87	1.92	-1.09	1.25	-1.16	1.45	-4.28	2.16	0.91	6.78	-2.45	-1.72
Output	-0.39	0.52	1.33	-1.34	0.89	2.37	1.17	-1.26	1.47	-3.84	2.04	1.58	5.49	-2.04	-0.82

Table A-2 --Continued

Industry:	(1) Agriculture and Mining			(2) Crude Petroleum and Refining			(3) Construction			(4) Textiles, Apparel and Leather			(5) Metals		
Period:	1982	1990	2000	1982	1990	2000	1982	1990	2000	1982	1990	2000	1982	1990	2000
(4) Low Investment Sensitivity															
Investment	0.61	1.98	3.57	0.09	3.05	5.50	-2.62	-1.92	1.91	-0.04	3.54	6.43	0.52	1.05	4.85
Profits	-0.48	1.71	-0.83	-2.53	6.29	5.75	2.68	-2.13	1.89	-5.71	5.25	6.70	6.48	0.78	3.59
Employment	-0.83	0.63	-2.17	-2.54	2.04	-0.64	2.13	-1.56	0.33	-4.57	2.17	1.02	6.90	-2.67	-2.35
Output	-0.37	0.36	0.96	-1.12	0.71	1.48	2.02	-1.64	0.29	-3.97	1.91	1.38	5.56	-2.25	-1.60

*All results are based on "moderate spending reduction" assumptions.

Table A-2 -- continued

Industry:		6 Machinery			7 Motor Vehicles			8 Misc. Manufacturing			9 Services			10 Housing		
Period:	1982	1990	2000	1982	1990	2000	1982	1990	2000	1982	1990	2000	1982	1990	2000
(1) Central Case																
Investment	1.32	0.28	4.55	-1.51	2.63	5.96	1.34	4.10	7.79	0.48	3.94	7.88	-5.25	-3.30	-1.79
Profits	9.27	-0.07	3.05	-2.88	3.67	5.44	-0.22	3.21	6.45	-1.77	3.67	6.96	-9.85	-0.22	3.05
Employ- ment	8.67	-3.11	-2.38	-3.39	1.63	0.88	-0.29	0.17	0.08	-1.19	0.44	0.31	-7.30	2.05	2.03
Output	6.93	-2.65	-1.66	-2.69	1.09	1.46	-0.34	0.26	0.97	-1.03	0.37	1.02	1.77	-2.94	-2.78
(2) No International Capital Mobility																
Investment	0.27	1.27	5.44	-2.24	3.52	6.41	0.49	4.95	8.19	-0.13	4.94	8.23	-5.41	-2.76	-1.70
Profits	8.59	0.42	4.11	-3.12	3.86	5.72	-0.66	3.57	6.82	-2.69	4.35	7.27	10.92	0.56	2.56
Employ- ment	8.73	-3.14	-1.71	-3.14	1.40	0.81	-0.22	0.10	0.14	-1.24	0.45	0.15	-7.50	2.26	1.28
Output	7.00	-2.70	-0.99	-2.48	0.92	1.54	-0.27	0.20	1.11	-1.06	0.30	0.99	1.86	-2.93	-2.44
(3) High Investment Sensitivity																
Investment	3.00	-0.17	5.92	-1.55	3.80	7.28	2.60	5.00	9.19	0.77	4.85	9.61	-7.63	-3.44	-1.35
Profits	8.81	0.10	3.90	-3.06	3.88	6.12	-0.42	3.33	7.09	-1.98	3.78	7.52	10.71	0.78	3.50
Employ- ment	8.50	-3.08	-2.08	-3.35	1.71	0.94	-0.25	0.17	0.11	-1.11	0.41	0.20	-7.66	3.03	2.25
Output	6.82	-2.67	-1.36	-2.77	1.21	1.74	-0.39	0.39	1.16	-1.03	0.34	1.11	1.73	-3.98	-2.81
(4) Low Investment Sensitivity																
Investment	0.10	-0.43	3.22	-1.66	1.60	4.71	0.49	2.91	6.32	-0.14	2.79	6.22	-4.20	-3.22	-2.27
Profits	9.22	-0.47	2.42	-2.88	3.35	4.85	-0.21	2.88	5.90	-1.71	3.24	6.23	-9.17	-0.79	2.57
Employ- ment	8.58	-3.22	-2.57	-3.43	1.59	0.84	-0.31	0.15	0.08	-1.19	0.49	0.40	-6.83	1.60	1.80
Output	6.83	-2.79	-1.97	-2.66	0.98	1.20	-0.33	0.15	0.76	-0.99	0.32	0.87	1.78	-2.32	-2.74

COMMENT

Robert E. Baldwin

This paper by Barry Eichengreen and Lawrence Goulder is excellent. In part one they manage in only about 30 pages to present a general survey of the trends in international competitiveness in the steel, textiles, automobile, and apparel industries and the various economic factors explaining these trends. These include the changes in the nature of foreign competition in these sectors, the behavior of their labor costs relative to each other and to foreign labor costs, the increases in U.S. import protection as these industries faced increasing competition from foreign producers, the efforts to introduce new technology to become more competitive, and the greater use of joint ventures by U.S. firms to increase their competitive abilities. I know of no other paper that matches this one for comprehensiveness and insights into the causes of the competitive problem in these industries.

In part two the authors utilize a computable general equilibrium model they have developed to assess the relative importance of the various causes for the decline in U.S. international competitiveness discussed in part one. In particular, using simulation experiments, they attempt to determine the importance of the Reagan administration's fiscal actions--increasing government expenditures and reducing government receipts as percentages of GNP--in accounting for changes in the U.S. trade balance and the relative price of the dollar.

In my comments I should like, first, to consider some of the possible implications of their tentative conclusion that the fiscal policies of the Reagan administration can account for only a small part of the dollar's appreciation in the early 1980s and thus in the relative decline in the international competitiveness of the steel, textile, auto, and apparel industries. Then I will move on to a discussion of the appropriateness of the government's trade-policy responses to the increase in foreign competitive pressures.

Rather surprisingly, Eichengreen and Goulder's model indicates the increase in the government budget deficit from $61 billion in 1980 to $176 billion in 1983 results in only about a 2% appreciation of the dollar, in contrast to an actual appreciation of 43%. Similarly, simulated exports and imports change by only -1.6% and +.4%, respectively, in contrast to actual changes of -10% and +8%, respectively. The factors they cite as causes of the actual sharp dollar appreciation, other than the budget deficit, are the shift toward tight monetary policy in this country that accompanied the fiscal expansion, tight fiscal policies in other OECD countries, safe haven demands for dollar-denominated assets, and the possibility of a speculative bubble.

Since they find the exchange-rate effect of U.S. fiscal actions to be very small, they presumably would find the effect of foreign fiscal policies small too, if they constructed the same kind of model for other OECD countries. Safe haven demands for dollars also do not seem to be a significant factor in explaining the dollar appreciation, since there was no economic or political event in OECD countries to account for a major loss in confidence in foreign currencies. Similarly, as the authors point out, the speculative-bubble explanation seems to apply in the post-1983 period, after the dollar had already appreciated significantly. This seems to leave tight U.S. monetary policies as the main cause of the sharp dollar appreciation and subsequent adverse impact on U.S. industry.

Tight monetary policy was, of course, a legacy from the Carter administration, which in the face of double-digit inflation selected an advocate of this policy, Paul Volcker, as head of the Federal Reserve System. But the Reagan administration strongly supported a continuation of this policy as the major means of reducing inflation, even at the cost of raising the unemployment rate from about 6% in 1979 to 9.5% in 1983. If the Eichengreen/Goulder model is correct, it would appear that the continued rise in nominal interest rates in the early 1980s, coupled with the slowdown in the inflation rate, was the major reason for the large inflow of foreign funds and consequent appreciation of the dollar. The adverse effect of the dollar appreciation on exports and its encouraging effect on imports significantly intensified the competitive problems of the basic industries studied by Eichengreen and Goulder.

An interesting policy issue to speculate on is whether a less vigorous pursuit of a tight monetary policy that slowed both the increase in interest rates and the reduction in the rate of inflation would have slowed the dollar appreciation and spared basic industries from the intense competitive pressures from foreign suppliers. Similarly, if the Federal Reserve had introduced tight monetary policies earlier in the 1970s, perhaps the sharp inflation that led to these policies later would not have occurred. These are the kinds of important policy questions on which computable general equilibrium models can provide valuable insights and I would urge the authors to introduce the monetary side into their models so that they can undertake simulation experiments on these kinds of questions.

Before leaving this topic, I think it is important to emphasize the appeal of the Reagan macroeconomic policies from a political economy viewpoint. By pursuing expansionist fiscal policies coupled with tight monetary policies, this administration has been able to maintain unemployment rates that compare favorably with those in the latter half of the 1970s and, at the same time, keep inflation rates at a low level. These two economic achievements are politically popular. An unpopular outcome was the adverse impact of the dollar appreciation on export-oriented and import-competing industries. Surprisingly, the Reagan administration's policies have not been blamed for this outcome. Instead, blaming unfair competition from foreign countries for our competitive difficulties has caught on in Congress and elsewhere. Thus, there is little political-economic pressure from interest groups who think they are hurt by these policies to change existing fiscal and monetary policy. Expansionary fiscal policy, tight monetary policy, and a tough trade policy have great appeal, and political leaders with relatively short time horizons will find it difficult to abandon such policies. Yet, their long-run effects could be highly adverse on many sectors of the economy because of the need eventually to earn an export surplus to service the U.S. debt.

As I stated earlier, I also want to elaborate briefly on the authors' section on the trade policy response of the U.S. government to the competitive difficulties of the basic industries they studied. As Eichengreen and Goulder document, the United States has introduced country-specific quantitative import restrictions in each of the four industries. Economists usually stress the adverse efficiency of these restrictions on world economic welfare: less efficient producers take over production from the more efficient producers. I want to emphasize a more nationalistic argument against quantitative restrictions (QRs) in general and country-specific QRs in particular. It is that such restrictions generally do not provide the degree of protection promised to workers and firms. They, therefore, fail to take steps to adjust to the import competition to the extent they otherwise would and suffer greater economic and social losses than they would under alternative adjustment procedures.

The major problem with selective quotas is that other foreign suppliers enter the market to replace the imports from the foreign supplier now subject to a quota. The U.S. effort to provide import relief to domestic shoe manufacturers by quantitatively limiting imports of nonrubber footwear from Taiwan and Korea in 1977 illustrates this point. Although the volume of imported nonrubber footwear from Taiwan and Korea declined from 206 million to 180 million pairs in the next year, imports from other sources increased from 160 million to 193 million pairs. The U.S. import share from all sources was at 51% in 1981, the last year of the import restraints, compared to 47% in 1876, the year prior to the restraint program.

The same problem has been evident in the textile and apparel industries. As production has shifted to noncontrolled countries, the government has been forced to negotiate bilateral quotas with one country after another. Over an extended period, workers in these industries have not received the protection they expected. Increased foreign production in noncontrolled sources has also occurred in the steel industry. In the auto industry the Japanese voluntary export restraints have been more effective in stimulating domestic production, but, as the authors point out, the industry is bracing itself for not just an increase in imports from Korea and Europe but from Brazil, Mexico, Taiwan, Malaysia, and Thailand.

Producing more expensive varieties of a traded item is another response of foreign suppliers to quantitative controls in contrast to percentage tariffs. It has been estimated that two-thirds of the real price increase in Japanese automobiles after the voluntary export restraint agreement was due to an increase in the quality of the Japanese cars imported. Since employment is positively related to the value of a car, this meant that U.S. employment in the industry increased less than one would expect just from the quantitative decrease in imports of autos from Japan. This upgrading phenomenon has also been observed as a response to QRs in the footwear, textile, and apparel industries.

Still another drawback of QRs, as typically used by the United States, is that the revenue, which would accrue to the U.S. government as taxes if tariffs rather than QRs were imposed, goes to foreigners as a windfall gain. It has been estimated that the U.S. loses over $9 billion in revenue because of this point--revenue that could be used to retrain workers and help them adjust to changed comparative cost circumstances.

Since it is clear that more U.S. industries will face increased competitive pressures from foreign suppliers in the future, it is essential that we formulate a more effective policy to meet the adjustment problems of workers and capital owners in the affected industries. To provide greater certainty in the adjustment process, I think abandoning country-specific protection and returning to the most-favored-nation principle is essential. Moreover, a means of protection that channels to the United States the windfall gains associated with protection is needed. This can be done by using tariffs or possibly by auctioning off quota rights. The drawback of the auction method is that the problem of quality upgrading that reduces the effectiveness of protection remains.

To reduce industries' ability to maintain protection more or less indefinitely rather than make the necessary adjustments that are the purpose of temporary protection, the public must have more information about the consumer costs of import protection. Also the government needs to experiment with several new adjustment-assistance proposals that may induce workers to seek new jobs or retraining more readily than have previous schemes. It is clear that our present response to the adjustment problems caused by the increased internalization of U.S. markets is quite inadequate.

3 POLICY IMPLICATIONS OF THE SLOWDOWN IN U.S. PRODUCTIVITY GROWTH

John W. Kendrick

Introduction

The productivity record since World War II for the United States and eleven other major industrialized countries is described in the first part of this paper. For the manufacturing sector, productivity changes in the twelve countries are linked to changes in unit labor costs and price levels, which are one of several major factors affecting international competitiveness. Next, the results of growth accounting studies are summarized with respect to the main causes of the higher productivity growth rates abroad than in the United States, the reasons for the slowdown in productivity growth in all of the countries after 1973 and for the partial recovery in U.S. productivity growth since 1981. An alternative analysis of the causes of productivity growth based on interindustry differences in productivity growth rates is also presented to supplement the macro-economic analysis.

These analyses serve as a background for discussion of various policy options for accelerating the recovery of productivity growth in the United States. This final section of the paper is organized around six major causal factors identified as significant in the growth accounting and interindustry studies.

The estimates of productivity for the United States and the other countries were prepared by the Bureau of Labor Statistics (BLS), U.S. Department of Labor. They relate to output per unit of labor input--real gross domestic product (GDP) per person employed, and output per labor hour in manufacturing. The reconciliation item between changes in so-called "labor productivity" and in "total factor productivity" is, of course, the rate of substitution of capital for labor (real capital per unit of labor weighted by the capital proportion of factor costs). The Bureau prepares estimates of capital inputs and "multi-factor productivity" only for the United States. But I shall refer to relative rates of factor substitution computed in earlier work I have done on international productivity comparisons.[1] I also rely on the earlier work, based on growth accounting, to explain the differences in rates of productivity growth between the United States and the other countries over the several subperiods. The U.S. industry productivity estimates are those prepared by the American Productivity Center and relate to both total productivity and labor productivity. There the role of increases in the capital/labor ratios in raising labor productivity is shown explicitly.

THE PRODUCTIVITY GROWTH RECORD 1950-86 BY SUBPERIOD

Rates of change in labor productivity in both the domestic economy and the manufacturing sector are shown in Table 3.1 for the United States and an average of the eleven other countries listed in Table 3.2. Note first that the rates of growth in manufacturing are about double the rates for the entire domestic economies. A couple of tenths of a percentage point of the

Table 3.1

United States and Eleven Other Countries*
Domestic Economies and Manufacturing Sectors:
Output and Output per Unit of Labor Input
(average annual percentage rates of change,
1950-1986 by subperiod).

	1950 1986	1950 1960	1960 1973	1973 1979	1979 1986	1985 1986
Real gross domestic product						
United States	3.2	3.3	3.9	2.5	2.3	3.1
11-nation average	4.1	4.9	5.1	2.7	2.1	2.6
Real GDP per person employed:						
United States	1.4	2.1	1.9	0.03	0.8	0.9
11-nation average	3.4	4.2	4.2	1.8	1.6	1.5
Manufacturing output:						
United States	3.2	4.8	2.3	1.9	2.2	2.8
11-nation average	5.4	6.7	6.3	1.7	1.6	1.5
Manufacturing output per labor hour						
United States	2.5	2.0	3.2	1.4	3.2	3.5
11-nation average	5.6	4.7	6.4	3.8	3.2	1.7

*The countries are listed in Table 3.2

Source: Bureau of Labor Statistics, U.S. Department of Labor.

difference reflects the gradual trend toward shorter working hours, since in the domestic economy the denominator of the productivity ratio is persons employed, while in manufacturing it is labor hours. More important is the fact that in real gross domestic product the output of general government and about a fifth of the private service sector is measured in terms of real labor inputs without allowance for productivity change. The rest of the difference reflects the fact that productivity growth in manufacturing was significantly higher than in non-manufacturing.

Over the entire period 1950-86 productivity growth in both manufacturing and the domestic economy as a whole was about twice as much in the other nations as in the United States. As a result, the productivity gap narrowed greatly. Using purchasing-power-parity exchange rates developed by the United Nations, the BLS calculations indicate that average real GDP per person employed increased from 44 percent of the U.S. level in 1950 to about 79 percent in 1986. (See Table 3.2.) Level estimates are not available for manufacturing, but the differential productivity growth rates indicate that the narrowing of the productivity gap there was as dramatic as in the domestic economies.

The patterns of productivity growth in both the domestic economies and the manufacturing sectors were similar across the several significant subperiods. Growth rates were relatively strong between 1950 and 1973. In the domestic economies they averaged about two percent a year in the United States and better than 4 percent in the other eleven countries. In manufacturing, they averaged about 2 1/2 percent in the United States and 5 1/2 percent in the others--less in the 1950-60 decade and more between 1960 and 1973, which implies some deceleration in non-manufacturing productivity after 1960.

Between 1973 and 1979, all countries underwent a marked deceleration in productivity growth rates. Real gross product per person in the United States showed virtually no gain, and the eleven-nation average gain fell by more than half to a 1.8 percent annual rate. Manufacturing productivity gains held up somewhat better, falling by less than half in the other countries on average, but by more than half in the United States to a 1.4 percent average annual rate.

In the final period 1978-86 the patterns diverge. Real gross product per person engaged in the U.S. domestic economy recovered to a nearly one percent growth rate, while in the other eleven nations the rate decelerated a

Table 3.2
Real Gross Domestic Product Per Employed Person
Comparative Levels in the United States and Eleven
Other Countries[1]

	(United States - 100.0)				
	1950	1960	1970	1980	1986
United States	100.0	100.0	100.0	100.0	100.0
11-country average	44.3	51.7	6.6	76.2	78.9
Canada	76.9	80.1	84.1	92.8	95.0
Japan	15.2	23.3	45.7	62.7	68.9
Belgium	46.9	50.3	62.2	79.7	81.3
Denmark	49.0[e]	53.	60.1	66.6	68.8
France	36.9	46.1	61.9	80.2	84.3
W. Germany	32.2	49.2	61.7	77.4	80.9
Italy	30.9	43.9	66.4	81.0	82.9
Netherlands	56.7	64.2	78.0	90.7	86.3
Norway	44.5	52.0	58.5	75.1	80.2
Sweden	44.0[e]	51.8	62.6	66.6	68.8
United Kingdom	53.8	54.2	57.9	65.8	70.4

[1]Based on purchasing-power-parity exchange rates.

[e]Extrapolated by the author

Source: Bureau of Labor Statistics, U.S. Department of Labor, unpublished tables dated August 1987.

bit further to 1.6 percent. The pickup in the United States was more dramatic in manufacturing where the average productivity growth came back to 3.2 percent a year, the same as the average rate of gain in the other countries which decelerated further. In the last year of the subperiod, 1986, U.S. manufacturing productivity increased by 3.5 percent over the previous year, double the average increase in the other nations.

Causes of the Differences in Productivity Growth by Subperiod

My discussion of causal forces behind the differences in productivity growth is based on the growth accounting analyses that Edward F. Denison and I have performed individually.[2] This approach involves assembling indicators of the causes of productivity growth and estimating their contributions to the growth rate in successive periods. Rather than reproduce the tables from our publications, I shall summarize the chief findings and add some qualitative observations.

In his international comparisons of the U.S. and seven OECD countries, which ended with 1962, Denison found that little of the significant narrowing of the productivity gap with the United States between 1950 and 1962 was due to a more rapid pace of technological advance except in France. Most of the more rapid productivity growth abroad could be accounted for by other factors, notably more rapid accumulation of fixed capital per worker, resource reallocations, economies of scale from rapid growth of domestic and international markets, and fuller utilization of capacity. In Japan, technological advance was greater than in the other O.E.C.D. countries and did contribute to narrowing the productivity gap. So also did a much more rapid decline in the average age of fixed capital goods.

My extension of the Denison model for the subperiod 1960-73 indicates that almost half of the narrowing of the productivity gap was the result of more rapid technological advance. Since research and development outlays (R&D) do not directly account for most of the differential,[3] it is my conclusion that it was mainly the result of "technological catch-up" with the United States. This conclusion is supported by considerable collateral evidence concerning factors promoting the diffusion of advanced technology such as patents granted and licensed, U.S. exports of R&D intensive goods,

U.S. direct investment abroad, particularly in manufacturing, and the increasing numbers of foreign students in American universities and engineering schools.

The other major factor promoting faster productivity growth in the other countries was the continuation of an almost one percent a year faster rate of substitution of capital for labor than in the United States. This was associated with a continued more rapid decline abroad in the average age of fixed capital stocks which contributed to technological gains. The higher rates of capital formation abroad was, of course, made possible by higher saving rates. (See Table 3.3) In 1973, the ratio of gross saving to GDP in the U.S. was about 20 percent. In Canada and the European countries (except the U.K.) it averaged nearly 25 percent, and in Japan exceeded 35 percent. On a net basis, U.S. saving was 11 percent, compared with 25 percent in Japan and about 15 percent in the other countries (except the U.K.). Savings in the U.K. were little higher than in the United States, as was its productivity growth. In most of the countries, saving rates increased between 1960 and 1973.

Small contributions to higher growth rates abroad were made by resource reallocations, slightly greater increases in the average education of the workforce, less negative effects of changes in the age-sex composition of the workforce, and greater economies of scale associated with a higher economic growth rate than in the United States. The latter effect was partially offset by a relative increase in the rate of utilization of capacity between 1960 and 1973 in the United States.

The marked slowing of productivity growth between 1973 and 1979 (which continued through the recession of 1982) was greater proportionately in the United States, but was more in percentage points of deceleration abroad. Capital/labor substitution declined both in the United States and abroad, but the decline was greater in the United States. The oil shock contributed to the slower growth of capital per worker directly by rendering some energy-intensive equipment obsolete, and indirectly by sparking greater inflation that eroded economic profit margins in most countries. The decline in saving rates after 1973, particularly net saving, is shown in Table 3.3.

Table 3.3

Ratios of Gross and Net Saving To Gross
Domestic Product; United States and Eight Other OECD
Countries (percentages, selected years 1960-1988)

	Gross Saving(Investment) Ratios				Net Domestic Saving Ratios			
	1960	1973	1979	1986	1960	1973	1979	1986
United States	18.7	20.3	20.9	18.3	9.2	10.9	8.4	2.5
8-country average	25.0	26.1	23.8	19.9	14.9	16.6	11.8	9.5
Canada	22.9	24.3	25.0	20.9	6.7	13.4	11.9	6.6
Japan	32.7	38.1	32.5	28.2	22.1	25.6	19.1	18.5
United Kingdom	18.6	22.1	19.9	17.3	9.7	13.6	8.7	6.0
France	24.8	27.8	23.7	19.0	16.7	18.9	13.4	7.7
W. Germany	27.4	25.3	23.5	19.3	21.1	16.3	11.4	11.1
Italy	28.7	27.1	24.3	21.2	18.9	15.3	14.4	11.0
Sweden	25.3	21.4	20.0	17.6	14.4	14.3	6.6	6.9
Belgium	19.3	22.7	21.5	15.8	9.3	15.4	9.1	8.5

Source: Organization for Economic Cooperation and Development

Note: Net domestic saving equals gross saving (investment)
less capital consumption, net foreign investment and
the statistical discrepancy.

The largest contributor to the slowdown appears to have been a diminished rate of technological progress, although it remained about one percentage point higher abroad than in the United States. It seems clear that the rate of technological catch-up with the U.S. was slowing, although the increase in real R&D outlays also decelerated abroad as it did in the United States. The average age of fixed capital goods was no longer dropping in most countries.

Economies of scale were presumably less abroad than in the United States as the rate of economic growth slowed more, as did rates of utilization of capacity, reflecting anti-inflationary macro-economic policies. Reallocation of labor no longer was a significant positive force in either area. The quality of labor continued to improve at similar rates here and abroad. The negative effect of government regulations on productivity as measured increased to about the same extent here and in the other eleven countries as a whole, contributing about 0.3 to the slowdown.

With respect to the 1979-86 subperiod, the table shows that in the domestic economies labor productivity growth decelerated a bit further for the eleven-nation average to a 1.6 percent annual rate, while in the United States it accelerated substantially to a 0.8 annual rate. In part, this was due to an accelerated rate of growth of the capital-labor ratio in the United States, and a further deceleration abroad. Also, changes in the age-sex mix of the labor force became favorable for the United States in the 1980s, and costs of regulatory compliance ceased rising in relation to GNP. For the business economies of both areas, the rates of growth of total factor productivity converged further, based on preliminary estimates. In manufacturing, the rates of labor productivity growth were the same from 1979 through 1986. This reflected deceleration abroad and a sharp acceleration in the United States--due in part to increased competitive pressures on managements from the appreciation of the dollar during the first half of the 1980's and disinflation domestically.

Preliminary extensions of my growth accounting analysis of the differences in productivity growth between the United States and the other countries for the subperiod 1979-86 indicates that the residual reflecting technological advance was significantly larger only for Japan, with the average for Canada and the European countries only slightly greater than that for the United States. This suggests that catch-up was of declining importance for technological progress in the other industrialized nations. After all, real GNP per person in most of the European nations was around 80 percent of that in the United States by the early 1980's, and in Canada it was 95 percent. In Japan it was still under 70 percent, although in an increasing proportion of manufacturing industries Japanese productivity was close to that in the United States, and had exceeded it in several.

Furthermore, by the 1970's, the proportions of GNP devoted to R&D in a number of other countries was close to the U.S. ratio, and had exceeded it with respect to civilian R&D in Germany and Japan. There was a marked increase in U.S. real R&D outlays beginning in the late 1970's, but the increases were about the same proportionately as in the European countries for which data are available, and less than the increases in Japan. It appears that innovational activity in the other countries is based increasingly on their own inventive resources, and to a decreasing extent on technology transfer from the United States. If this is so, the era of significantly faster productivity growth in other industrialized countries than in the United States may well have ended around 1980, assuming no marked relative changes in proportions of GDP devoted to R&D. In the United States, there is a potential for greater productivity gains stemming from technology transfer from abroad as scientific and technological knowledge there exceeds ours in more fields.

Other Competitive Considerations

The relationship between relative productivity changes and international competitiveness of national economies is much more tenuous than is the relationship between relative industry changes in productivity and the competitiveness of the goods produced in the various industries. In the business (enterprise) sectors of national economies, relative productivity changes are only one element in changes of general price levels expressed in terms of a particular national currency. Relative overall productivity performance can be overshadowed by the other elements affecting relative price movements.

In the first place, unit labor costs, the major element in price, are the quotient of average compensation per hour or per worker and labor productivity. Hence, a country with relatively low increases in productivity may also have relatively low increases in unit labor costs in terms of its national currency if its increases in average labor compensation are also low compared with its major trading partners. This was true for the United States compared with most of the other eleven countries shown in Table 3.4 for the subperiods 1960-73, 1973-79, 1979-85, and 1986. In 1986, the situation became doubly favorable in that the United States had the largest annual productivity gain and the lowest increase in average hourly labor compensation. As a result, it was the only country of those shown in the table that had a decline in unit labor costs. The decline appears to have continued in 1987.

Over intermediate and longer time periods, there is a strong positive correlation between relative changes in unit labor costs and in prices. Deviations can occur if non-labor costs change significantly as a fraction of total costs, which happens mainly in the short-term and mainly with respect to prices of raw materials and, cyclically, profit margins.

The other major variable that affects unit labor costs and prices of exports and imports in terms of U.S. dollars (or any other currency) is changes in exchange rates. From 1960 through 1973, the currencies of most of the other countries shown in the table appreciated relative to the dollar. This gave the United States a further advantage in its relative unit labor costs and prices which rose less than those of any other country except Canada whose dollar depreciated against the U.S. dollar.

The situation changed very much during the 1978-85 subperiod when the dollar reversed course and appreciated against all the other currencies--significantly so relative to all except the Canadian dollar and the yen. As a result, unit labor costs in terms of U.S. dollars dropped in all the countries except Japan and Canada, and only in Canada did unit labor costs rise a bit more than the 3.7 percent average rate of increase in the U.S. manufacturing sector (see Table 3.4C). The real net export balance began falling in 1981, and became increasingly negative from 1983 through the summer of 1986.

A reversal followed the peaking of the value of the dollar in the first quarter of 1985. Between 1985 and 1986, the dollar had depreciated substantially against the currencies of all other countries shown in Table 3.4D except Canada. The United States was the only country to show an actual decline in unit labor costs in manufacturing. In all the other countries except Canada, the increases in unit labor costs measured in U.S. dollars were large. Although final data for 1987 are not yet in, it is apparent that the favorable trends for the United States continued as the dollar declined further in currency exchanges.

The major reason the U.S. trade balance has not improved more since the J-curve effect began to take hold is that prices of our imports have not increased nearly in proportin to the appreciation of foreign currencies. Their exporters have absorbed part of the appreciation through reducing profit margins in order to try to hold on to the important U.S. markets. Also, the currencies of some of our trading partners not shown in the Table, such as Taiwan and Korea, have appreciated only modestly.

This analysis underscores the point that good productivity performance is but one of three major elements in bolstering the international competitiveness of an economy. The second element is the containment of factor price increases to the zone of productivity advances in order to avoid serious inflation of unit costs and prices. The third element is to maintain the foreign exchange value of the currency within an equilibrium range to avoid marked fluctuations in net exports of goods and services, and to pursue reciprocity in other terms of trade. The United States has made significant progress on all three fronts, although the value of the dollar has only recently reached a level from which more substantial reductions in the trade deficit seem likely to occur over the next several years.

INTERINDUSTRY DIFFERENCES IN PRODUCTIVITY GROWTH

Macro-economic changes in productivity are a weighted average of productivity changes in the component industries of an economy. This section presents and discusses estimates of productivity changes between 1948 and 1986 by subperiod for 31 industry groups of the U.S. business economy. The focus is on variables associated with the interindustry differences in productivity growth in order to supplement the macro-economic analysis of causal factors in the preceding section and provide further background for discussion of policy options.

It should first be noted that since relative industry changes in productivity exhibit a strong negative correlation with relative price changes by industry, they are an important element in explaining patterns of international trade. But productivity estimates are not available for most of our trading partners in the same degree of industry detail as for the United States. Nor is it our assignment to analyze international differences in

Table 3.4

Productivity, Wage-Rates, and Unit Costs
Twelve Countries, 1960-1986 By Subperiod
(Average annual percentage rates of change)

Country	Output/ Labor Hr.	Avg. Hour. Pay	Unit Labor Costs National Currency	Unit Labor Costs U.S. $	Exchange Rate (rel. to U.S. $)
Part A 1960-73					
United States	3.2	5.0	1.8	1.8	---
Canada	4.5	6.2	1.6	1.4	-0.2
Japan	10.3	15.1	4.3	6.6	2.2
Belgium	6.9	11.0	3.8	5.8	2.0
Denmark	6.4	12.2	5.5	6.6	1.0
France	6.5	10.0	3.3	4.1	0.8
W. Germany	5.8	10.3	4.3	8.0	3.5
Italy	7.3	13.6	5.9	6.4	0.5
Netherlands	7.4	12.9	5.2	7.7	2.4
Norway	4.3	10.0	5.4	7.2	1.7
Sweden	6.4	10.5	3.9	5.3	1.3
United Kingdom	4.3	9.3	4.8	3.7	-1.0
Part B 1973-79					
United States	1.4	9.5	8.0	8.0	---
Canada	2.1	11.9	9.7	6.8	-2.6
Japan	5.5	12.8	6.9	10.8	3.6
Belgium	6.2	14.0	7.4	12.5	4.8
Denmark	4.2	14.0	9.4	11.9	2.3
France	5.0	16.3	10.7	11.5	0.7
W. Germany	4.3	9.5	4.9	11.6	6.3
Italy	3.3	20.6	16.7	10.0	-5.8
Netherlands	5.5	11.6	5.8	11.7	5.6
Norway	2.1	13.4	11.1	13.4	2.1
Sweden	2.6	14.2	11.2	11.5	0.3
United Kingdom	1.1	19.3	17.9	15.1	-2.4

Table 3.4 continued
Productivity, Wage-Rates, and Unit Labor Costs
(Average annual percentage rates of change)

Country	Output/ Labor Hr.	Avg. Hour. Pay	Unit Labor Costs National Currency	Unit Labor Costs U.S. $	Exchange Rate (rel. to U.S. $)
Part C 1979-85					
United States	3.1	6.9	3.7	3.7	---
Canada	1.7	8.7	6.9	4.2	-2.5
Japan	6.1	5.0	-1.0	2.5	-1.5
Belgium	5.3	7.7	2.3	-9.1	-11.1
Denmark	1.6	7.9	6.2	-5.5	-11.0
France	3.8	12.5	8.4	-4.3	-11.7
W. Germany	3.0	5.8	2.8	-5.0	-7.6
Italy	3.6	16.7	12.6	-2.0	-13.0
Netherlands	4.4	5.2	0.8	-7.3	-8.1
Norway	2.6	9.9	7.1	-1.9	-8.4
Sweden	3.3	9.7	6.2	-5.5	-11.0
United Kingdom	4.6	11.1	6.2	-2.1	-7.9
Part D 1985-86					
United States	3.7	3.3	-0.4	-0.4	---
Canada	-0.2	3.9	4.1	2.4	-1.7
Japan	2.8	3.5	0.7	42.6	41.7
Belgium	2.6	3.7	1.1	34.3	32.8
Denmark	1.3	5.9	4.5	36.8	30.9
France	1.9	4.5	2.5	32.9	29.7
W. Germany	1.5	4.7	3.1	39.8	35.5
Italy	1.2	4.3	3.0	31.9	28.0
Netherlands	-0.3	2.4	2.7	39.2	35.5
Norway	-0.6	9.7	10.4	28.2	16.1
Sweden	0.2	7.4	7.2	29.3	20.7
United Kingdom	3.5	7.4	3.7	17.4	13.1

Source: "Trends in Manufacturing Productivity and Labor Costs in the U.S. and Abroad," <u>Monthly Labor Review</u>, Dec. 1987, U.S. Dept. of Labor.

productivity growth on an industrial basis. Yet our analysis of the reasons for the inter-industry differences in the United States will suggest reasons why the same industries would show different rates of productivity growth internationally and thus affect trading patterns.

Table 3.5 shows average annual percentage rates of change from 1948 to 1986 in real gross product per labor hour (so-called "labor productivity") and in "total factor productivity" (TFP). TFP is the ratio of real product (value added) to the associated inputs of labor and capital (including land) as estimated by the American Productivity Center. It measures the net saving of resource inputs per unit of output as a result of cost-reducing technological innovations and the other variables discussed above. Labor productivity additionally reflects the substitution of capital for labor in production as explained above. The increase in real capital per unit of labor input is shown in the last column of the table. The change in capital/labor substitution equals the difference between the TFP and labor productivity rates of changes. Thus, for the business economy as a whole, the difference between the rates of change in the two productivity ratios rounds to 0.5 percent a year (2.2-1.7) which roughly equals the 1.9 percent a year average increase in the capital/labor ratio times the capital share of factor income which averaged over 25 percent.

Note that capital grew faster than labor in all the industry groups, so TFP grew at a lesser rate than labor productivity in all. Further, there is a positive correlation between rates of change in capital per unit of labor and labor productivity in the various industries. This means there is less dispersion in rates of change in TFP than in rates of change in labor productivity. Both ratios showed declines over the 38-year period 1948-86 in only one industry--contract construction--and the small negative probably reflects difficulties in measuring output in custom building. Labor productivity growth ranged up to over 5 percent in farming and telecommunications, and in manufacturing the range was from one percent in primary metals to between 4 and 4 1/2 percent a year in textiles, electrical machinery and chemicals. Service sector productivity grew less rapidly than productivity in tangible goods industries.

Table 3.5
U.S. Business Economy by Major Industry Groups
Total Factor Productivity, Real Product Per Labor Hour
and Capital/Labor Ratios, 1948-1986
(Average annual percentage rates of change)

	Real Gross Product	Total Factor Prod.	Labor Prod.	Capital-Labor Ratio
U.S. Business Economy	3.2	1.7	2.2	1.9
Goods Sector	2.6	2.1	2.7	2.3
Farming	1.4	3.6	5.0	4.2
Mining	1.3	0.7	1.8	4.1
Construction	1.7	-0.3	-0.2	1.3
Manufacturing	3.3	2.1	2.7	2.0
Food	2.5	2.5	3.0	2.1
Tobacco	0.8	0.4	2.6	4.5
Textiles	2.9	4.0	4.5	2.3
Apparel	2.2	2.1	2.4	2.6
Lumber	2.4	2.4	3.0	3.7
Furniture	2.7	1.5	1.8	2.0
Paper	3.7	2.0	2.7	2.8
Printing & Pub.	2.8	0.9	1.2	2.0
Chemicals	5.3	3.0	4.0	2.7
Petroleum	2.6	0.8	3.2	3.6
Rubber	4.8	1.8	2.2	2.1
Leather	-1.1	1.0	1.5	3.3
Stone, Clay & Glass	2.2	1.4	2.0	2.4
Primary Metals	-0.2	0.2	1.0	3.9
Fabricated Metals	2.7	1.4	1.8	3.2
Machinery-except electrical	4.6	2.8	3.5	3.3
Electrical Machinery	6.5	3.6	4.3	3.7
Trans. Equipment	3.9	1.9	2.5	2.6
Instruments	5.9	3.0	3.5	2.4
Misc. Manufacturers	2.7	2.5	3.1	3.5
Service Sector	3.7	1.4	1.9	1.3
Railroads	-1.0	2.5	3.2	2.5
Nonrail Transportation	2.2	0.8	1.0	1.2
Communications	6.4	3.8	5.4	5.0
Publications	5.6	3.3	4.4	2.5
Trade	3.7	2.0	2.4	3.0
Finance & Insurance	4.1	0.4	0.9	2.9
Real Estate	3.7	0.7	1.2	0.5
Services	4.1	0.6	0.9	1.0

Source: American Productivity Center

In particular, finance, insurance, real estate and private services proper (FIRES) averaged only about one percent productivity growth per year. Again, there was some downward bias in this sector due to difficulties in measuring output in the FIRES group. The reason the table is confined to the business sector is that real product in the non-business domestic sectors (households, nonprofit institutions, and general government) is measured entirely in terms of labor input without allowance for productivity change. But gross business product comprises about 80 percent of total GNP according to the official estimates.

Estimates of rates of change in real gross product originating (GPO) in each of the 31 industry groups are shown in the first column. To obtain GPO, the real expenditures for intermediate products consumed in production by each industry are deducted from the real value of gross output. Hence, economies in use of intermediate inputs (materials, supplies, energy and other purchased services) are reflected in GPO since such economies cause real GPO to rise faster than gross output. For some purposes it is desirable to relate gross output to all inputs, intermediate as well as factor services, since the derived total and partial productivity ratios would explicitly show the savings in intermediate inputs as well as in labor and capital usage as a result of technological progress. Also, all inputs are substitutable for each other when relative input prices change. But for present purposes, the GPO estimates, which are more readily available suffice.

There is a positive correlation between relative industry changes in output and in productivity. This is a reciprocal relationship. On the one side, there are the effects of economies of scale on productivity. On the other side, above-average productivity gains stimulate sales and output, with some exceptions, through their dampening effect on price increases. The notable exceptions are farming and the FIRES group, where weak price elasticities are outweighed by income elasticities working in the opposite direction.

There is considerable variability in rates of productivity change measured across subperiods bounded by business cycle peaks, as shown in Table 3.6. There, the first subperiod covers several cycles including the 1966-67 mini-recession. There was strong growth in the 1948-53 subperiod, a slowing in both of the subperiods 1953-57 and 1957-60, then a resumption of strong advances in labor productivity in the first half of the 1960s. There was a further moderate slowing of productivity gains between 1965 and 1973,

Table 3.6

U.S. Business Economy by Major Industry Groups
Real Gross Product Per Labor Hour
1948-1986 by Subperiod
(Average annual percentage rates of change)

	1948-86	1948-73	1973-79	1979-86
U.S. Business Economy	2.2	2.8	0.6	1.4
Goods Sector	2.7	3.2	0.5	2.5
Farming	5.0	4.7	3.1	7.9
Mining	1.8	4.1	-6.9	1.7
Construction	-0.2	0.8	-2.1	-2.1
Manufacturing	2.7	2.8	1.4	3.5
Food	3.0	4.0	0.8	2.9
Tobacco	2.6	4.0	2.5	-2.3
Textiles	4.5	4.1	6.6	3.8
Apparel	2.4	2.3	3.4	1.7
Lumber	3.0	3.3	2.6	1.7
Furniture	1.8	2.1	2.8	-0.1
Paper	2.7	3.2	1.3	2.5
Printing & Pub.	1.2	2.0	0.0	-0.8
Chemicals	4.0	4.9	2.5	2.2
Petroleum	3.2	4.3	0.0	1.8
Rubber	2.2	2.4	-0.3	3.4
Leather	1.5	1.6	0.7	1.8
Stone, Clay & Glass	2.0	2.2	1.3	1.7
Primary Metals	1.0	1.5	-2.1	2.1
Fabricated Metals	1.8	2.0	0.6	2.4
Machinery-except elec.	3.5	1.9	0.9	11.6
Electrical Machinery	4.3	4.1	4.3	4.6
Trans. Equipment	2.5	3.2	0.6	1.2
Instruments	3.5	3.6	2.9	3.6
Misc. Manufacturers	3.1	3.2	0.8	4.9
Service Sector	1.9	2.5	0.7	0.7
Railroads	3.2	3.9	1.1	2.6
Nonrail Trans.	1.0	1.5	1.7	-0.8
Communications	5.4	6.0	4.3	4.1
Publications	4.4	6.3	0.3	1.2
Trade	2.4	2.9	0.8	2.0
Finance & Insurance	0.9	1.4	-0.1	0.2
Real Estate	1.2	2.0	-0.2	-0.6
Services	0.9	1.3	0.2	0.1

Source: American Productivity Center

followed by the drastic productivity slowdown of 1973-79 which enveloped all but 5 of the 31 industry groups. Based on a detailed analysis Frank Gallop concluded that "the slowdown in aggregate productivity growth is not the result of shifts in economic activity from high-to low-productivity-growth sectors or the market system's failure to reallocate resources... The evidence suggests that the decline in sectoral productivity growth has been both widespread and substantial, thereby lending support to a sectoral-neutral industrial strategy."[4]

The slowdown was followed by the less widely recognized pickup in productivity gains after 1979 (particularly after 1981) in which about two-thirds of the industry groups participated. The average for the business economy picked up from a 0.6 percent average annual gain between 1973 and 1979 to a 1.4 percent rate 1979-86. The year 1986 was not yet a cycle peak, but the average gain was already half-way back to the long-term rate of growth of 2.2 percent a year. This improvement was due in part to policy measures taken since 1979. It would seem quite feasible to restore U.S. productivity growth back at least to the long-term trend rate if further favorable policy measures are taken along the lines discussed in the final section.

To come to the causal analysis, a variety of variables affecting relative productivity changes have been identified by multiple regression analyses. The variables enumerated below do not all appear to be significant in any one regression. Some of the independent variables are correlated with each other; e.g. average education of workers and outlays on research and development (R&D). But in alternative specifications, only one of the interrelated variables shows up as significant. The following variables have proved to have a significant positive relationship with relative industry rates of productivity change in labor productivity in one or more of the regressions performed by the present writer and others:[5]

* ratios to sales of research and development outlays, direct and indirect
* changes in R&D ratios
* rates of growth of real fixed capital per worker
* average education per worker
* proportions of non-production workers and of females in total industry employment
* variability in layoff rates,
* economies of scale.

Variables that were negatively associated with industry rates of productivity change include:

* the amplitude of cyclical changes in output
* average hours worked per week
* changes in average hours
* the percentage of workers belong to unions
* days lost because of strikes
* changes in industry concentration ratios, and
* changes in the female proportion of the workforce.

The results of the interindustry studies generally confirm the importance of the causal variables identified by macro-economic growth accounting--in particular, capital/labor substitution, R&D and technological progress, human investments, and changes in composition of the workforce. The effects of reallocations of resources among industries would show up only in the macro-economic analyses, of course. On the other hand, institutional variables such as concentration and unionization are easier to capture in cross-sectional analyses due to wide differences among industries in contrast to slow changes over longer time periods in the economy as a whole.

Students of productivity are generally agreed on the causal factors that are significant in explaining growth. They differ chiefly in the weights they assign the underlying variables. That is why I have not quantified in this paper the percent contributions it has been estimated that the various factors made to productivity changes over the several subperiods. Comparisons have been made of the estimates prepared by a number of investigators which may be consulted by those who are interested.[6] The important thing has been to identify the most significant variables as background for formulating policy options to stimulate productivity advance.

POLICIES TO PROMOTE PRODUCTIVITY AND TECHNOLOGICAL ADVANCE

The policy options discussed in this section are general and not industry or technology specific. Most economists agree that a targeted industrial policy is unlikely to do a better job than markets do in allocating investment funds. Indeed, political pressures can produce government industrial policies that misallocate resources and weaken productivity growth. Our focus is on measures that could be taken mainly by the federal government to stimulate advances in technological knowledge and their application to the ways and means of production in the directions judged to be most productive by the players in the enterprise economy.

In 1980, I wrote a paper, "Policies to Promote Productivity Growth" which contained 99 policy options.[7] Some of the measures have since been adopted, and others proposed. Here, I suggest a number of measures not yet enacted under six major headings that correspond to the major causal forces behind productivity advance: economic expansion, increasing technological knowledge, saving and tangible investments, human investment, labor efficiency, and government roles not covered in the previous points.

Volume Factors

Rates of change in output and in productivity show a strong positive correlation, reflecting both economies of scale and of utilization. Economies of scale are a function of the rate of growth of output, since growth opens up opportunities for greater specialization of people, plants, and equipment, and spreads overhead functions over more units. Cyclically, expansion from lower rates of utilization of capacity towards most efficient rates boost productivity and vice versa. In general, innovation is easier when output is expanding smartly than when it stagnates or declines. The reduction in economic growth from 1973 to 1981 was a cause as well as an effect of the productivity slowdown.

The economic expansion beginning in late 1982 proceeded rapidly through mid-1984, boosting productivity growth to near 3 percent a year, then slowed drastically through 1986. Rates of utilization of industrial capacity declined, and so did productivity gains. It would be desirable if aggregate demand in the economy increased at least as fast as the expansion of productive capacity, estimated at between 3 and 4 percent a year. Marked cyclicality of demand slows the growth of capacity and productivity. The slowdown for the decade beginning in 1973 was due in part to the most severe contractions since World War II in 1974 and 1982.

The objective of relatively steady growth of real GNP around the "natural" rate of unemployment requires appropriate macro-economic policies. Since the unemployment rate in 1987 averaged 6.2 percent--about one percentage point above the natural rate below which wage and price inflation tends to accelerate--growth could probably proceed at near 4 percent for a couple of years without a serious heating-up of inflation. Then growth should slow somewhat, reflecting the slower growth of the labor force projected for the 1990's, and the assumed leveling of unemployment at between 5 and 5 1/2 percent of the civilian labor force. It is important that unemployment not fall below the natural rate if a renewed wage-price spiral is to be avoided. We have already seen the depressing effect of accelerating inflation on capital formation and productivity. Strong increases in capital formation are a key element in obtaining strong growth of real GNP and productivity.

An important part of the stronger expansion should be a continuation of the faster growth of exports than of imports in real terms that started in the fall of 1986, due in part to the major decline in the foreign exchange value of the dollar since early 1985. To promote continued significant declines in the trade balance, continued reductions in the federal deficit are needed. Also, U.S. foreign economic policy must not only seek to maintain an equilibrium value of the dollar; it must encourage stronger economic growth of our major trading partners, and continue negotiations for freer and fairer trading rules and practices on their part and ours. It should be noted that exports of services as well as of goods have benefited from the improved trade balance.

The expansion of the share of the service sector in the economy has tended to reduce cyclical fluctuations. This makes the task of macro-economic policy easier. On the other hand, the shift to services tends to lower the growth of productivity and productive capacity, which underlines the importance of seeking measures that will accelerate productivity growth in services as well as in goods production.

Promoting Technological Knowledge

In the modern era, the fountainhead of scientific knowledge and technological advance is investment in research and development (R&D). Ratios of R&D, direct and indirect, to sales within manufacturing industries are significantly correlated with rates of productivity advance. The great increase in the ratio of national R&D to GNP from a small fraction in 1919 to near 3 percent in the mid-1960's was a major reason for the acceleration in productivity growth after World War I. The subsequent decline in the ratio until the latter 1970s is cited as a reason for the productivity slowdown after

1973, given the lags between R&D and commercial effects. The increase in both business and government financed R&D since the late 1970s contributed to the pick-up in productivity growth after 1982, particularly in manufacturing where the bulk of R&D is concentrated.

It is important that R&D continue to increase at least in line with GNP, and preferably somewhat faster if the supply of scientists and engineers permits without undue inflation of salaries. Most of the increase in government financed R&D has been for national security purposes. As that increase slackens it will be desirable to increase financing of applied R&D for civilian purposes. Recent increases in funding of basic research, and the planned doubling of appropriation requests for the National Science Foundation over the next five years, are welcome developments.

The passage of a 25 percent incremental R&D tax credit in 1981 helped maintain the strong increases in business R&D. It was extended in 1986, but at a 20 percent rate, and the extension was for another temporary, three-year period. This may have contributed to a slowing of increases in business R&D. We recommend that the credit be increased to at least 25 percent, the definition of R&D be broadened, and include facilities and equipment, the increments be computed on a stable base (not a moving average), and that the credit be made permanent since R&D programs require long-term planning.[8]

Patent, copyright, trademark and trade secret protection has been strengthened pursuant to recommendations in the 1985 report of the President's Commission on Industrial Competitiveness. The protection of intellectual property has been raised to a priority concern in the coming round of multilateral trade talks. Some people recommend lengthening the period of patent protection from 17 to 20 years, or otherwise compensating for delays in commercialization of potential inventions because of federal regulations. There is also a need to strengthen the Patent and Trademark Office to improve search capabilities and reliability of patent grants.

The Committee for Economic Development (CED) recommends that when two or more inventors claim the same improvement, "the nation should change to first-to-file system, whereby the first inventor to file a patent application will receive the patent."[9] This would prevent extended delays in the issue of patents over which there are controversies. The public would benefit from early publication of the patent disclosure. A personal right of use could be preserved for anyone who had invented first and was in process of commercialization. The CED also believes that the government should consider permitting firms to write off expenditures for the purchase of patent rights or other externally designed innovations. This would encourage technology transfers more than the requirement that purchase of a patent be capitalized and depreciated over its useful life.

Serious considerations should be given to the proposals in the President's Competitiveness Initiative based on recommendations of his Commission.[10] Among the initiatives are the following:

    1. Establishment of new university-based, interdisciplinary science and technology centers that will perform research in areas that contribute to U.S. competitiveness (including services).

    2. Creation of a technology share program involving multi-year, joint basic and applied research with consortia of U.S. firms and universities.

    3. Initiation of an exchange program between scientists and engineers in the public and private sectors.

    4. Improved industry access to federal science and technology efforts to increase transfers, and accelerate the spin-off of defense technologies to the private sector.

    5. Programs to increase scientific literacy.

The National Cooperative Research Act of 1984 removed antitrust barriers to joint research. More than 40 consortia have notified the Department of Justice and Federal Trade Commission that they intend to take advantage of the new opportunities. It is important that companies in both goods and service industries take full advantage of these and related initiatives.

Saving and Investment

The significant positive correlation between rates of change in real capital per worker and output per worker obtains in international, interindustry, and intertemporal comparisons. This is not just a matter of the quantity of capital goods, but also their quality, since new plant and equipment are carriers of cost-reducing technological innovations. The volume of business investment depends on expected rates of return, and on the cost of capital, particularly interest rates which interact with saving rates. Saving is the ultimate constraint on the volume of investment that can be undertaken.

Table 3.7
Flow Of U.S. Net Saving and Investment

(percentage of GNP)

	1981	1986	1987[a]
Net private domestic saving	6.6	5.3	4.3
State and local government surpluses	1.1	1.3	1.0
Less: Federal budget deficit	2.1	4.8	3.5
Net domestic saving available for private investment	5.6	2.0	1.8
Plus: Net inflow of foreign saving	-0.1	3.4	3.4
Net private domestic investment	5.5	5.4	5.2

[a]First half of 1987.
Source: On the Capital Formation Front, November-December 1987, American Council for Capital Formation, Washington, D.C.

There is a growing consensus among economists that income taxes have a negative effect on saving and investment. Income taxation drives a wedge between the returns earned by investment and the income accruing to investors. It also drives a wedge between market rates of interest and the interest received by savers. Another way of expressing the negative influence of income taxation on saving and investment is that it represents double taxation of saving if that income is taxed and so it is the income from the investments into which savings flow.

From this point of view, the reductions in both corporate and personal income tax rates in the tax acts of 1981-82 and 1986 should have had a positive effect on saving and investment, other things equal. But the elimination of the investment tax credit and the accelerated cost recovery system in the 1986 Act resulted in a drop of business investment between the last quarter of 1985 and the first quarter of 1987, contributing to sluggish economic growth. In my view, consideration should be given by Congress to restoration of an investment tax credit.

More fundamentally, it will be desirable to further de-emphasize income taxation, or eliminate it, and to substitute consumption-based taxes. The crucial importance of increasing domestic saving is apparent from Table 3.7. Since 1981, the ratio of net private domestic saving to GNP has tended down. The increase in the federal budget deficit through 1986 caused net domestic saving available for private investment to decline much more sharply. Only the big increase in the net inflow of foreign saving has prevented net private domestic investment from declining significantly as a percentage of GNP. Economists at the Brookings Institution have made a good case for a consumed income tax.[11] A value-added tax is also neutral with respect to saving and consumption decisions, but appears to be politically unpopular. In the meantime, it would be desirable if the double taxation of dividends were eliminated, and tax-deferred savings plans liberalized.

An unfortunate aspect of the Tax Act of 1986 was the increase in capital gains taxation beginning in 1987. Business investments and formation of new businesses are undertaken in part in hope of realizing capital gains in the future. Capital gains taxation reduces that incentive. One attractive proposal for reducing capital gains tax rates is to reduce the capital gains on which taxes are levied to the extent that the price level (as measured by the consumer price index) had risen between the dates of purchase and sale of the assets.

With respect to interest rates, the most effective way to hold them down or reduce them further at this time is through continued reductions in the federal deficit. Government deficits absorb funds that would otherwise be available for private investment, and competition between business and governments in the money markets keeps interest rates higher than they would be if budgets were balance. Monetary policy should not be overly stimulative, however, because of the inflationary potential. But it can at least be neutral in view of the remaining slack in the economy at this time.

Human Investments

Growth accounting studies show that increases in average education and training of the workforce contributed about 0.7 percentage points to the 2.2 percent increase in labor productivity between 1948 and 1985.[12] On a cross-sectional basis, as noted earlier, there is a significant positive correlation between rates of change in average education and output per labor hour by industry. Along with tangible investments and technological advance, education and training rank among the most important forces promoting productivity advance. It is basic to producing the scientists, engineers, and business managers who are responsible for innovation, and to preparing the labor force generally to operate an increasingly complex technology.

It is important that both public and private outlays for education and retraining continue to increase as a ratio to GNP. The 1985 report of the President's Commission on Industrial Competitiveness made several recommendations in the human resources area. Among these were:

(1) Expansion of federal training and assistance programs for displaced workers;

(2) Greater funding of engineering education, as through expansion of NSF engineering centers;

(3) Sustained federal support for a program of basic and prototype research in educational software through NSF and the Department of Labor; and

(4) More effective dialogue among government, industry, labor, academia, and other interested parties to develop consensus on educational and other measures to increase competitiveness.

A task force headed by the Secretary of Labor concluded that government programs to deal with displaced workers should be consolidated and funding for retraining nearly tripled. The President's FY 1988 budget provided almost $1 billion for worker adjustment assistance, well above last year. The President's Initiative recommends an $800 million program under the Job Training Partnership Act to provide summer jobs and remedial education and skills training for disadvantaged youths.

The Administration's 1988 budget requested an increase of $600 million for an experimental loan program to allow students to borrow more money than now permitted. but this comes at the expense of proposed reductions in vocational education and funding of higher education.

An older proposal is for tuition tax credits. Another is for development and diffusion of new educational methods and technologies by the National Institutes of Education, along with research to determine those which are most effective in facilitating learning. Increasing emphasis should be placed on life-long learning. The National Academy of Engineering has stressed this with respect to the need for continuing education of engineers.[13]

Health is another form of human investment. Here the emphasis must be on development of new and more effective medical technology and treatments, and on continuing education of the public in healthful life styles. Further increases in the productivity of health care facilities are essential to bringing down their relative costs.

Labor Efficiency

With a given level of technological knowledge, the actual output of individuals and organizations depends on the degree of efficiency relative to a sustainable optimum. In the short run, the productivity of most individuals and groups can be increased significantly with proper leadership, motivation, and inputs of brain and brawn.

Over the past decade, there has been a major shift in management philosophy and practice in many firms and other organizations from the old "Theory X" military, chain of command model to "Theory Y", involving participative management and the use of employee involvement (EI) systems. Some of the EI plans, such as quality circles and joint labor-management productivity teams, do not involve special financial incentives. Others, such as

Scanlon or Rucker plans, Improshare, productivity gain-sharing and profit-sharing plans, do incorporate financial incentives with rewards linked to performance. A number of surveys of EI systems, both with and without financial incentives, indicate that managers believe they have significantly enhanced productivity.[14]

Installation and maintenance of EI plans, and systems for tying pay to performance, depend on management initiatives, of course. But both the Department of Labor and the Federal Mediation and Conciliation Service have staffs that can assist in developing cooperative efforts of management and labor to promote productivity. They can also assist in union-management negotiations involving the moderation or elimination of restrictive work rules or jurisdictional conflicts that impair productivity. The longer-term payoff of EI plans come when they elicit worker suggestions for cost-reducing innovations in the workplace.

An Executive Order issued by OMB in February 1986 requires federal agencies and departments to develop productivity measures, to set up systems for involving workers in efforts to improve productivity, and to use productivity improvement goals in budgeting. These efforts are being reviewed and evaluated by the General Accounting Office, which is in a position to recommend modifications to make them more effective. The federal government is prepared to help state and local governments in similar efforts. Getting "more bang for the tax buck," or spending fewer bucks for the bang in government is a significant element in raising national productivity.

Governmental Policies

In providing the legal framework within which private enterprises operate, government plays an important role in the productivity of the business economy. The aggregates and composition of government expenditures and revenues also have a significant impact on the private economy. We have discussed the effects of taxation and the government surplus or deficit on private saving and investment. Likewise, the proportions of government expenditures devoted to public investments in infrastructure and in intangibles such as R&D, education, training, and health affect the productivity of the private economy. Many economists think that a separate capital budget for government would help focus attention on the importance of public investment. Certainly, strict cost-benefit analyses should be applied in selecting specific investment projects to be undertaken.

Of particular concern to business has been the proliferation of governmental regulations since 1970. The costs of complying with regulations increase inputs while the presumed benefits do not increase output as measured; hence, social regulations are believed to have played a part in the productivity slowdown. It is important that the Administration persevere in its efforts to rationalize the regulatory process, requiring early public involvement before enacting new regulations; coordination of agency activities; tightening of procedural requirements for evaluative choices of proposed regulations and re-evaluation of existing regulations; and improving evaluation methods. Where regulations are found to have negative impacts, provisions for minimizing or eliminating such impacts should be made. Agencies must be held accountable for the claimed benefits relative to costs and risks. Performance should be reviewed regularly, and failure to achieve satisfactory results would be case for deregulation or substitution of alternative procedures.

Regulations should be goal-oriented rather than specifying means. Agencies should try to compensate for the greater relative burdens placed on small firms by regulations. They should study and take account of the impact of their actions on the international competitiveness of the U.S. economy, and the effects on innovation, productivity, and costs.

The effects of reducing or eliminating economic regulations in a variety of industries has had salutary effects, including increases in productivity.[15] Technological advances have increased competition within and among industries, and it is to be hoped that the movement towards reducing or eliminating economic regulations will continue.

Even in the public utility area, increased use of automatic cost adjustments to rates charged could reduce the frequency of costly and time-consuming rate-of-return hearings before regulatory commissions, and the possible erosion of profit margins before rate adjustments are permitted. It would be particularly beneficial if regulators permitted above-average rates of return for telecommunications, electric and gas and other regulated companies that demonstrate superior productivity performance as a result of innovations that cut costs while maintaining or improving quality of service.[16]

In recent years, antitrust laws have been interpreted more broadly by the Justice Department and Federal Trade Commission to permit mergers that would increase efficiency without restraining trade. This contributes to productivity growth. But it remains essential that mergers and collusive activity of firms that would lead to monopolistic pricing be prohibited. Healthy competition is a powerful force promoting innovation, productivity advance, and reduction of real costs per unit of output. The effective functioning of the U.S. economy depends on its maintenance.

CONCLUDING OBSERVATIONS

The productivity gap between the United States and other industrialized countries has narrowed greatly since 1950. This was the result of much stronger rates of productivity growth abroad until recently due to two major factors. One was a stronger increase in real capital stocks and services per employed person in the other countries than in the United States. This reflected generally higher rates of saving and investment abroad as a result of more favorable taxation and other macro-economic policies in other countries, although it is possible that the basic propensity to save is lower in the United States. The other factor was a more rapid rate of technological progress abroad reflecting importantly the catching-up in an increasing number of industries with more advanced U.S. technologies. In some industries, foreign firms have surpassed U.S. technology which opens up increased opportunities for reverse technology transfer.

By the 1980's, there was a noticeable tendency towards convergence of productivity growth rates, as they improved in the United States while decelerating a bit further abroad, particularly in manufacturing, following the 1973-79 slowdown. The chief factor reducing the international competitiveness of U.S. products was the appreciation of the dollar during the first half of the 1980's. But since 1985, continued significant improvements in U.S. productivity combined with a major depreciation of the dollar against a trade-weighted average of other currencies has begun to reduce the trade deficit in real terms.

Improvements in U.S. competitiveness can continue if:

(1) the foreign exchange value of the dollar stabilizes in an equilibrium range, which may be near at hand in early 1988, although some economists think some further moderate depreciation may be necessary;

(2) there is further liberalization of international economic relations to reduce restrictions on U.S. exports, and promote a stronger expansion of world trade generally;

(3) avoidance of a renewed spiral of wage-price inflation in the United States while maintaining growth of aggregate demand more or less in line with expansion of productive capacity; and

(4) further improvement in U.S. productivity performance at least back to the long-term trend rate of 2.2 percent a year in real gross business product per labor hour, together with improved quality in both products and productive processes.

It is to the last point that our discussion of policy options was addressed, although it is clear that higher rates of productivity advance will help combat inflation and promote stabilization of the foreign exchange value of the dollar. In that connection, it is likely that there will be further convergence in rates of productivity growth between the United States and other industrialized nations, contributing to the expansion of world output and trade to the benefit of all.

The competitive market system is the most important spur to productivity improvements, with profits the incentive and reward for successful cost-reducing and market-expanding innovations. Further, current and prospective profit rates are important for effective allocation of resources among alternative uses. It is basic that governmental measures should facilitate and enhance the smooth functioning of the market system. Reduction or removal of economic regulations and barriers to international trade, and rationalization of social regulations work in that direction. It makes sense for the government to facilitate the mobility of resources in response to the continual changes in technology, resources and tastes that continually take place in a dynamic economy. Programs for training and retraining of workers help reduce the costs to particular individuals which result from the economic progress of the nation at large. But economists generally regard it as a bad idea to help declining firms and industries escape from the rigors of competition that promotes rising productivity by shifting resources to more efficient uses.

The market system works best when displaced resources can be absorbed in expanding industries as aggregate demand increases in line with capacity growth. But those responsible for macro-economic policies must be vigilant not to drive unemployment below the natural rate if accelerating wage and price inflation is to be avoided.

Relatively steady, non-inflationary economic growth provides a favorable background for private saving and investment, which is central to productivity advance. In this paper, we have used the term investment broadly to include R&D, education and other human investments as well as plant and equipment and other tangible investments. As stressed earlier, saving and investment will be stimulated if the government moves further away from income taxes towards consumed-income taxes in the process of reducing the federal deficit. In addition, measures that penalize saving should be eliminated, and measures taken to encourage investment, but on a sector-neutral basis. Where externalities are significant, as in basic research and education, direct government support is warranted. Government support for emerging technologies and industries should be given only in the rare instances when a very strong case can be made that private initiative would be inadequate and that the probabilities of a successful outcome are high.

Given the fact that human capital is greater than nonhuman capital, it is important that the work-force use its capabilities fully. Experience with employee involvement programs and productivity gain-sharing programs has been favorable. These have the added virtue of increasing the flexibility of labor costs on the downside, which helps hold occasional recessions to modest proportions. Incentives and entrepreneurial activity, with its unavoidable uncertainties, can be enhanced by more favorable treatment of capital gains, as proposed in the body of the paper. After all, it is the entrepreneur who has the ultimate responsibility for the innovations that are the major force behind advances in productivity and economic welfare.

Notes

1. John W. Kendrick, "International Comparisons of Recent Productivity Trends," in William Fellner, ed., Essays in Contemporary Economic Problems, Demand, Productivity and Population (Washington: American Enterprise Institute, 1981), pp. 125-170.

2. Edward F. Denison, Why Growth Rates Differ, and Denison and W. K. Chung, How Japan's Economy Grew So Fast (Washington: The Brookings Institution, 1967 and 1976) and Kendrick, op. cit.

3. Nestor E. Terleckyj, Effects of R&D on the Productivity Growth of Industries (Washington: National Planning Association, 1974; and John W. Kendrick, "Differences Among Industries in Productivity Growth; Overview of a Fall 1984 AEI Conference." Studies in Economic Policy Occasional Paper (Washington: American Enterprise Institute, November 1986).

4. See Frank M. Gollop, "Analysis of the Productivity Slowdown: Evidence for a Sector-Biased or Sector-Neutral Industrial Strategy," in William J. Baumol and Kenneth McLennan, Productivity Growth and U.S. Competitiveness, A Supplementary Paper of the Committee for Economic Development (New York: Oxford University Press, 1985), pp. 180-1.

5. See John W. Kendrick, ibid., and "Interindustry Differences in Productivity Growth," A Study in Contemporary Economic Problems, 1982 (Washington: American Enterprise Institute, 1983).

6. See Edward N. Wolff, "The Magnitude and Causes of the Recent Productivity Slowdown in the United States: A Survey of Recent Studies," in Baumol and McLennan, op. cit., pp. 29-57.

7. John W. Kendrick, "Policies to Promote Productivity Growth," Agenda for Business and Higher Education (Washington: American Council on Education, 1980), pp. 44-135.

8. Kenneth M. Brown, The R&D Tax Credit, Issues In Tax Policy and Industrial Innovation (Washington: American Enterprise Institute, 1984).

9. Productivity Policy: Key to the Nation's Economic Future, A Statement by the Research and Policy Committee of the CED (Washington: Committee for Economic Development, April 1983).

10. See America's Competitive Crisis: Confronting the New Reality, A Report by the Council on Competitiveness (Washington: Council on Competitiveness, April 1987).

11. See Barry P. Bosworth, Tax Incentives and Economic Growth (Washington: The Brookings Institution, 1984).

12. Edward F. Denison, Trends in American Economic Growth, 1929-1982 (Washington: The Brookings Institution, 1985), and John W. Kendrick, "Productivity Trends and the Recent Slowdown: Historical Perspective, Causal Factors, and Policy Options," in Contemporary Economic Problems 1979, William Fellner, Ed. (Washington: American Enterprise Institute, 1979), pp. 17-69.

13. Federal Actions for Improving Engineering Research and Education (Washington: National Academy of Engineering, 1986).

14. People and Productivity, A Challenge to Corporate America (New York Stock Exchange Office of Economic Research, 1982). A new survey has been conducted during 1987 by the American Productivity Center, Houston.

15. Elizabeth E. Bailey, "Price and Productivity Change Following Deregulation: The U.S. Experience," Economic Journal, March 1986, pp. 1-17.

16. See William J. Baumol and Kenneth McLennan, Productivity Growth and U.S. Competitiveness, op. cit., pp. 204-206; also John W. Kendrick, "Efficiency Incentives and Cost Factors in Public Utility Automatic Revenue Adjustment Clauses," Bell Journal of Economics, Spring 1975, pp. 299-313.

COMMENT

C. A. Knox Lovell

Introduction

It is a great pleasure to have the opportunity to comment on a paper of John Kendrick, a scholar whose work has put him at the forefront of the productivity growth field for three decades. Beginning with his monumental Productivity Trends in the United States (1961), his work has had a profound influence on the way I and others approach a wide variety of issues related to productivity growth, its measurement, and its management. I am not a bit surprised that this paper meets the high standards we have come to expect from Kendrick. It is rich in international historical insight; it reflects great care in collecting, analyzing, and reporting a wealth of statistical data; and it is full of provocative policy prescriptions which, if followed, might significantly enhance this nation's productivity growth.

Kendrick makes many points in this wide-ranging paper, but three points stand out. First, he provides an authoritative history of the post-WWII productivity record in the U.S. and eleven other inudstrialized nations. Briefly, that history shows U.S. productivity growth lagging behind that of the other nations through the 1970's, and surpassing that of the other nations during the most recent decade. It also shows the well-known slowdown in productivity growth that plagued all twelve nations from the mid-1970's through the mid-1980's. These findings are fairly robust with respect to different data bases and different definitions of "productivity," although their sensitivity to different time periods is unknown. The second point Kendrick makes is one that is often overlooked in both the productivity growth literature and the international competitiveness literature. It is that productivity growth is but one of three components of a nation's international competitiveness. The other two being resource price movements and exchange rate behavior. Thus a nation's menu of policy options aimed at improving its competitiveness in international markets is not limited to those options that would increase its rate of productivity growth. Indeed Kendrick's third contribution is to provide a menu of policy options aimed at all three components of competitiveness.

I agree with much of Kendrick's history (although not all of it, as I shall explain below), and I find many of his policy recommendations sensible (although in some cases the likelihood of enactment is minimal). Accordingly, I wish to focus my substantive remarks on three features of productivity growth that are generally underappreciated and deserving of closer scrutiny. The first two features are mentioned, but given insufficient emphasis, by Kendrick. The third he ignores, and is the source of my disagreement with a portion of his history.

A Brief Digression

Before proceeding to these three features of productivity growth, however, I want to engage in a brief rhetorical digression intended to put Kendrick's contribution in proper perspective. Why do we study productivity growth? Because it is an important problem, of course. Why is it important? Because the growth of a nation's total output of goods and services is equal to the growth of its resource base plus the growth in the productivity of its resource base. If a nation's resource base is stagnant, then output growth requires that its resources become more productive. Productivity growth thus contributes to the ability of a nation to increase its provision of goods and services, and so to its ability to increase the standard of living of its citizens. This is very important indeed. However, we observe the outputs a nation produces, and we observe the resources it consumes, but we do not directly observe its productivity growth. As a practical matter, then, productivity growth is calculated as a residual, the difference between the growth in a nation's outputs and the growth in its resource use.

Many years ago Moses Abramowitz (1956) quite properly called the calculated residual "a measure of our ignorance." It consists of outputs we have overlooked or have not measured accurately, and resources we have overlooked or have not measured accurately, and improvements in technology, and changes in the efficiency with which resources are allocated, and a host of other elements about which we are so ignorant as to be incapable of accurately assigning them to "output growth" or "resource growth" or "productivity growth." Abramowitz was right, as Robert Solow (1957) so convincingly demonstrated by his inability to account for 7/8 of economic growth in the U.S. economy over the period 1909-49.

Abramowitz's prescient characterization of Solow's result created an occupation, the decomposition of the unexplained residual in growth accounting. During the past thirty years more and more goods and services and resources have been measured with increasing accuracy, and the unexplained residual has been shrinking toward a more accurate measure of true productivity growth. We remain ignorant, but far less so today than three decades ago, due to the work of such scholars as Edward Denison (1974), Dale Jorgenson and Zvi Griliches (1967), and many others, but most especially John Kendrick.

Having attempted to put Kendrick's work into perspective, I now turn to my list of three underappreciated features of productivity growth.

The Efficiency With Which Resources are Allocated

When a nation's resources are inefficiently allocated, its output of goods and services is less than the maximum allowed by its resource base. Improvements in the efficiency of resource allocation lead to increased outputs obtainable from given resources, and can be thought of as contributing to productivity growth. The question is which misallocations can be corrected at what gain in productivity.

In the 1950's and 1960's attention centered on what I call "macro-inefficiencies," those due to monopoly and monopsony power, regulatory distortions, trade restrictions and the like. The problem was that these inefficiencies were thought to reduce output by very little, much less than one per cent by most accounts (Arnold Harberger (1954) and other studies cited by Harvey Leibenstein (1966)). Thus not only were these inefficiencies deeply imbedded in our economy and hence difficult to eliminate, their elimination did not offer much in the way of increased productivity growth.

So in the last decade or so attention has switched to what I call "micro-inefficiencies," those occurring within private businesses and public organizations. Interest in micro-inefficiencies has been spurred in part by the dim prospects for increased productivity growth through reductions in macro-inefficiencies, and, as Kendrick notes, by an interest in Japanese management philosophy and practice as a possible way of improving productivity growth at the level of the individual production unit. In the private sector, a myriad of participative management and employee involvement systems have been instituted. In the public sector, the Reagan administration is attempting to enact legislation that would require federal organizations to develop productivity measures that would be used in the federal budget allocation process. This would be exceedingly difficult, in light of federal accounting practices and the problems involved in defining, much less measuring, the outputs of many federal organizations, but it is a well-intentioned step in the right direction. Again in the public sector, recent interest in privatization has resulted in part from a widespread belief in the superior productivity of private providers of many services currently being provided by the public sector (both philosophy and case studies are surveyed in Thomas Borcherding, Werner Pommerehne and Friedrich Schneider (1982)).

My own belief, based on the pioneering work of W.E.G. Salter (1960), which inspired the work of Harvey Leibenstein (1976) and many others, is that there exist sufficient micro-inefficiencies in both sectors to inspire confidence that their reduction can offer substantial increases in productivity at the national level. However since maximum attainable productivity levels are rarely if ever known, we need to focus on the dispersion of observed productivity levels beneath what Salter called "best practice" levels. The little empirical evidence that does exist suggests that reducing this dispersion by bringing inferior performers up toward best practice standards can yield large increases in overall productivity. Most of this evidence is European, however, where research is facilitated by the fact that government/business/academic cooperation is closer there than it is in the U.S. (the benefits of this cooperation for analyzing business productivity are illustrated in the work of Finn Førsund and Lennart Hjalmarsson (1984)). One very promising joint venture in the U.S. is government funding, through the Bureau of the Census, for construction and scholarly study of a Longitudinal Establishment Data (LED) file covering production activities of thousands of manufacturing establishments. Although it covers only the private manufacturing sector, the LED file should yield insights into the distribution of productivity and the phenomena with which superior performance is associated. Similar data files for the private non-manufacturing sector and the public sector would be even more valuable to scholars, executives and policy-makers.

The Effects of Social Regulation

Social regulation, as provided for example by the Environmental Protection Agency (EPA) and the Occupational Safety and Health Administration (OSHA), is intended to improve the quality of our lives. It is achieved at a cost, of course, since it forces business to reallocate resources away from the provision of goods and services toward the provision of cleaner environments and safer workplaces. The regulated reallocation of resources reduces conventionally measured productivity, often by large amounts. Frank Gollop and Mark Roberts (1983), to cite but one example, report that environmental controls reduced the rate of productivity growth in the U.S. electric power industry over the 1974-79 period by 0.59 percentage points to -1.35 percent per year. Numerous other studies reach similar conclusions; a good collection of studies is Thomas Cowing and Rodney Stevenson (1981).

By any number of criteria the effect of social regulation on productivity growth is a problem worthy of further investigation. It is important enough to attract roughly equal attention from the American Enterprise Institute and the Brookings Institution. Social regulation is applied unevenly across nations, and across industries within nations, and hence has differential impacts on measured productivity growth rates that are dangerous to ignore. It may be efficiently or inefficiently structured and operated, and so may have unnecessarily severe impacts on productivity, a point raised by Robert Crandall (1981). It is important by virtue of its sheer magnitude; in 1985 approximately $74 billion was spent on pollution abatement and control alone in the U.S.. Interestingly enough, of that total just over $1 billion was allocated to regulation and monitoring, and just over $2 billion was spent on R&D (Survey of Current Business, May 1987).

Despite the enormous importance of social regulation and its impact on productivity growth, I wish to offer the not exactly novel suggestion that the impact is overstated, perhaps grossly so. The overstatement is easy to explain and difficult to quantify. In redirecting resources from the production of measured outputs to the reduction of unmeasurable or unmeasured disamenities, social regulation reduces conventionally measured productivity growth. But conventional measures of productivity growth surely understate "true" measures of productivity growth if we value clean air and water, and safe workplaces. More work needs to be devoted to the valuation of these nonmarket amenities if we are to obtain a more accurate picture of the effect of social regulation on productivity growth. One such effort, an attempt to measure "Net Economic Welfare" by William Nordhaus and James Tobin (1972) has not attracted the following it deserves.

The Effects of Temporary Equilibrium Phenomena

The strong deceleration in productivity growth in the U.S. and the other industrialized nations that occurred during the 1973-82 decade has puzzled scholars ever since its discovery. Kendrick cites several sources for the slowdown: a decline in capital/labor substitution, obsolescence of energy-intensive capital brought on by the oil price shocks, a diminished rate of technological progress, and the deleterious effects of government regulations.

I have no quarrel with any of these explanations; each contributed to the slowdown. What I wish to suggest is that the slowdown has been exaggerated. The latest research on both sides of the Atlantic argues persuasively that the reported slowdown in productivity growth overstates the true slowdown, perhaps by as much as 65%. Three exceptionally lucid presentations of this point are by Ernst Berndt and Melvyn Fuss (1986), Margaret Slade (1986), and John Muellbauer (1987); many more could be cited.

Again the basic idea is fairly easy to explain but difficult to quantify. Most productivity growth calculations assume that producers are in full long-run equilibrium when, as the result of business cycle phenomena, they are in fact in short-run temporary equilibrium. The corrections that have been made in an effort to correct for temporary resource price changes and underutilization of production capacity have been inappropriate. Making the appropriate corrections leads to the conclusion that reported declines in productivity growth have been overstated because growth in resource usage has been overstated, the latter being attributable to the fact that underutilized resources have been valued by their market prices rather than by their (lower) shadow prices. Presumably the same line of reasoning could be used to show that conventionally measured productivity growth is overstated when an economy is recovering from a recession, as in Kendrick's final 1979-86 period.

The conclusion is that cyclical variation in measured productivity growth is overstated. The problem is to determine by how much, and why.

A Final Remark

Kendrick has provided us with an informative overview of the recent productivity growth record of the U.S. and eleven other major industrialized nations, as well as a long menu of policy options to improve productivity growth in the U.S.. For his thought-provoking analysis we are in his debt. In my comments I have attempted to focus fairly narrowly on three relatively underdeveloped issues related to productivity growth and its accurate measurement. We could hope for no better outcome than to have this list of neglected issues attract the attention and considerable skill of John Kendrick.

REFERENCES

Abramowitz, M. (1956), "Resource and Output Trends in the United States Since 1870," American Economic Review 46:2 (May), 5-23.

Berndt, E.R., and M.A. Fuss (1986), "Productivity Measurement With Adjustments For Variations in Capacity Utilization and Other Forms of Temporary Equilibrium," Journal of Econometrics 33:1/2 (October/November), 7-29.

Borcherding, T.E., W.W. Pommerehne and F. Schneider (1982), "Comparing the Efficiency of Private and Public Production: The Evidence From Five Countries," Zeitschrift fur Nationalokonomie 42, Supplement 2, 127-56.

Cowing, T.G., and R.E. Stevenson, editors (1981), Productivity Measurement in Regulated Industries. New York: Academic Press.

Crandall, R.W. (1981), "Pollution Controls and Productivity Growth in Basic Industries," Chapter 13 in Cowing and Stevenson (1981).

Denison, E.F. (1974), Accounting For U.S. Economic Growth, 1929-1969. Washington, D.C.: Brookings Institution.

Førsund, F.R., and L. Hjalmarsson (1984), Analysis of Industrial Structure: A Production Function Approach. Stockholm: IUI.

Gollop, F.M., and M.J. Roberts (1983), "Environmental Regulations and Productivity Growth: The Case of Fossil-fueled Electric Power Generation," Journal of Political Economy 91:4 (August), 654-74.

Harberger, A. (1954), "Monopoly and Resource Allocation," American Economic Review 44:2 (May), 77-87.

Jorgenson, D., and Z. Griliches (1967), "The Explanation of Productivity Change," Review of Economic Studies 34:2 (July), 249-82.

Kendrick, J.W. (1961), Productivity Trends in the United States. Princeton: Princeton University Press.

Leibenstein, H. (1966), "Allocative Efficiency vs. 'X-Efficiency'," American Economic Review 56:3 (June), 392-415.

Leibenstein, H. (1976), Beyond Economic Man. Cambridge: Harvard University Press.

Muellbauer, J. (1987), "Aggregate Production Functions and Productivity Measurement: A New Look," presented at Conference on Measurement and Modelling in Economics, Nuffield College, Oxford, UK, May 21.

Nordhaus, W. and J. Tobin (1972), Is Growth Obsolete?. New York: National Bureau of Economic Research.

Salter, W.E.G. (1960), Productivity and Technical Change. Cambridge: Cambridge University Press.

Slade, M.E. (1986), "Total Factor Productivity Measurement When Equilibrium is Temporary: A Monte Carlo Assessment," Journal of Econometrics 33:1/2 (October/November),

Solow, R.M. (1957), "Technical Change and the Aggregate Production Function," Review of Economics and Statistics 39:3 (August), 312-20.

4 THE TAX REFORM ACT OF 1986 AND ECONOMIC GROWTH

Patric H. Hendershott

Introduction

Both economic growth and productivity growth declined sharply in the 1970s. For the 1959-73 period, real output and productivity growth averaged over four and two percent, respectively; since 1973, each has been one and a half percentage points less.[1] Productivity growth has rebounded in recent years, but substantial concern still exists regarding the long-run output path of the United States' economy. Major tax reform has the potential to alter that path significantly.

In the long run, the growth rate of an economy is determined by the rates of technological progress and of growth in labor supply. These rates are difficult to influence with tax policy. In the short run, however, economic growth depends on changes in both the capital/output ratio and the level of work effort, variables that can be affected by tax policy. Moreover, a higher growth rate for even a few years translates into a higher level of output, or output path, over time.

The 1986 Tax Act will have a negative impact on economic growth. A revenue-neutral tax reform that raises the standard deduction and personal exemption cannot, in general, increase the bundle of goods one can purchase with an additional hour worked. Cuts in marginal personal tax rates can be achieved by broadening the tax base and shifting the tax burden to businesses. However, while the after-tax wage will increase, so will the after-tax cost of

---

I thank Sheng Hu, James Mackie, Joel Slemrod, and, especially, Yolanda Henderson for useful discussions. The research reported here is part of the NBER's research program in Taxation. Any opinions expressed are those of the author and not those of the National Bureau of Economic Research.

goods consumed, both currently and in the future, and thus work effort is unlikely to rise. Similarly, a tax reform that shifts the tax burden from labor and existing capital to new investments will likely lower saving and reallocate capital away from industrial uses. While the Tax Act will increase the efficiency of business investment, the potential efficiency gains are so small that actual gains will be swamped by the direct effect of a smaller business capital stock.

My analysis is divided into three basic parts and a conclusion. The basic parts discuss the likely impact of the 1986 Tax Act on work effort, saving, and the quantity and quality of business investment. I begin each part with an analysis of potential gains from tax changes and then examine the 1986 Tax Act.[2] The conclusion summarizes the earlier analyses and briefly discusses future policies to stimulate economic growth.

TAX REFORM AND LABOR SUPPLY

One touted benefit of tax reform is greater work effort in response to a reduction in marginal tax rates on labor income. While economists disagree on many issues, there is substantial consensus that labor supply, especially that of secondary workers, is highly responsive to increases in the return from work. Because greater labor supply expands national income, many advocated tax reform on this basis.

Potential Gains

A revenue-neutral, distributionally-neutral tax reform can lower marginal tax rates on labor income in just three ways: by broadening the tax base, by shifting the statutory tax burden from households to businesses, or by reducing the effective progressivity of the tax burden. However, an increase in labor supply is likely only if the tax rate reductions are achieved by reducing the system's effective progressivity because only in this case will most workers be able to purchase more goods for an extra hour of work (Browning and Browning, 1985, and Slemrod, 1987). In the other two cases, the price of some goods, as well as the after-tax wage rate, will rise, making an increase in the real return from work uncertain.

Base broadening consists of either taxing previously untaxed sources of income or disallowing existing deductions. If the previously untaxed sources are labor income, including them in the tax base and using the revenues to lower statutory tax rates doesn't lower effective marginal tax rates and won't increase labor supply. A change from a 50 percent tax rate applied to 50 percent of income to a 25 percent rate applied to all income reduces the incentive to take income in the previously nontaxed form but shouldn't affect labor supply. In either case, 25 percent of a marginal dollar of income goes to the Treasury and 75 percent is retained by the worker.

Disallowing existing deductions or taxing previously untaxed capital income and using the funds to lower tax rates also probably doesn't increase labor supply. The incentive to work depends on the amount of goods one can purchase with an additional hour of work, not just the after-tax wage rate. While a cut in marginal tax rates increases after-tax income from the hour of work (and thus the reward in terms of goods not included in the base broadening), disallowing deductions increases the "after-tax" prices of goods that were previously tax favored, reducing the reward for work in terms of these goods. Thus the quantity of goods one can purchase with the greater after-tax wage does not necessarily increase, and no increase in hours worked should be expected.

To see this point more clearly, consider some specific deductions. The largest is that for home mortgage interest. The revenue raised from disallowing this deduction would allow a significant reduction in marginal tax rates and thus would increase the after-tax wage. But the annual cost of financing housing would rise from the after-tax mortgage rate, say three-quarters of 10 percent, to the full before-tax rate, 10 percent in our example. Would people work harder in response to an increase in their after-tax marginal wage rate, even though the cost of a major component of their consumption has increased even more sharply? Probably not.

What about the deductibility of state and local income, sales or property taxes? First of all, loss of the state and local income tax deduction would not necessarily permit lower marginal total tax rates when federal, state and local taxes are considered. For example, a 30 percent federal rate along with a fully deductible 5 percent state rate gives a 33.5 percent total rate. Removing the deductibility and lowering the federal rate to 28.5 would leave the total rate unchanged. Second, while loss of the sales tax deduction would allow a reduction in marginal tax rates, for itemizers it would also raise the effective price of goods subject to the tax (and for nonitemizers it wouldn't raise any revenue). Third, loss of the property tax deduction would raise the effective price of municipally-provided services that property taxes finance. Because the prices of some goods and services rise, even a higher marginal after-tax wage rate need not trigger greater work effort.

But what if lower household tax rates are achieved by shifting the tax burden to business? This doesn't change the argument because business taxes are ultimately paid by households, either as lower wages (if an increase in profit taxes is shifted to workers) or higher prices. If excise taxes are increase (or become nondeductible), the price of current consumption rises; if profit taxes are increased and capital income (rents, dividends, interest, etc.) falls, the price of future consumption (the after-tax return to saving) increases. In either case, greater labor supply would not be likely to follow; a higher price would tend to offset the positive incentive of a higher after-tax marginal wage rate on work effort.

Browning and Browning (1985) make the case with a simple example. If the tax liability under both old and new law is $3,000 on an income of $30,000 and $5,000 on an income of $40,000 (the tax change is distributionally neutral), then the effective marginal tax rate applied when income rises from $30,000 to $40,000 is 20 percent for both laws. And work effort will likely be the same even if one law has low marginal rates applied to a broad base and the other has higher rates applied to a narrower base.

The 1986 Tax Act

Slemrod (1987) suggests two means by which the distribution of tax burdens within income classes could be altered so as to increase labor supply within the context of a revenue neutral reform: reductions in the minimum standard deduction and in the personal exemption. Both would increase marginal tax rates (from zero to the lowest marginal rate) for a subset of taxpayers who paid no taxes prior to the reductions but now would pay taxes. The revenue pick-up from these taxpayers would allow the marginal tax rates of all others to be cut. The positive labor response of the latter group should roughly offset the negative response of the former group. In addition, though, the reduction in standard deduction and/or personal exemptions of those who previously paid taxes would allow a further reduction in their marginal tax rates, and this should then lead to an increase in total labor supply.

Lowering the personal exemption has another advantage. Because the number of personal exemptions per tax return rises with income, marginal tax rates could be reduced without changing the distribution of the tax burden by income class.

The 1986 Tax Act will not provide labor supply incentives through either of these channels. In fact, the 1986 Act went in the opposite direction, raising the standard deduction and personal exemption in order to increase fairness. Moreover, partly because of these changes the Tax Act is likely not distributionally neutral. In fact, if the increased corporate taxes are assumed to fall entirely on capital income recipients, then the tax burden is noticeably shifted from those earning under $50,000 to those earning over (Aaron, 1987). A reduction in labor supply should be expected from such a redistribution.

In a widely cited study (possibly because it seems to be the only one), Hausman and Poterba (1986) report that the Tax Reform Act would increase labor supply of the average married man by 0.9 percent, and they conjecture that this is a good estimate of the aggregate effect on male labor supply. They then consider the average married woman married to the average married man and compute a 2.6 percent increase in labor supply. Here they are reluctant to extrapolate to total female labor supply.

Slemrod (1987) contends that this analysis is flawed because the underlying model is based on a two-good world where the two goods are leisure and a non-tax-preferred consumption good. Thus the negative effect on labor supply of disallowing deductions--the increase in after-tax prices of previously tax-favored consumption goods--is ignored by definition. How the shift in the tax burden from household to business--the increase in the price of future consumption--is handled is unclear, but it too appears to be ignored. While the "average" married man may not hold large quantities of stock (although he must have stock in his retirement savings), one would not want to extrapolate from such an individual to the full population. Thus the Hausman-Poterba study does not really conflict with the prior argument that the 1986 Tax Act will not increase labor supply.

SAVING

Another possible benefit of tax reform is greater saving in response to lower tax rates on capital income. Economists are in less agreement on the sensitivity of saving to increases in its net return than they are on the responsiveness of labor supply to increases in the return to work. I begin with a general discussion of economists' views on this issue and then turn to the specifics of the 1986 Tax Act as it affects first personal saving and then corporate and foreign saving. Assuming the Tax Act is revenue neutral, changes in total saving will occur only if private or foreign saving change.

After-Tax Returns and Personal Saving

Most economists believe personal saving to be relatively insensitive to net returns to saving. While economists have constructed models in which saving is highly sensitive (Summers, 1981a), alternative models give a small sensitivity (Evans, 1983). Moreover, econometric studies generally report low responses. Boskin's (1978) widely cited study reports an interest-rate elasticity of 0.2 to 0.6; more recently, Hall (1985) finds virtually no response. A major difficulty with all empirical studies is the measurement of the after-tax return (von Furstenburg, 1981). With so many alternative saving vehicles, with widely varying taxation and risk, how this return should be measured is far from obvious.

Because of the measurement problems, many economists look directly to historic periods where net rates of return clearly changed for evidence on the sensitivity. The first half of the 1980s is just such a period. The 1981 Tax Act both cut marginal tax rates and greatly expanded the scope of tax-preferred retirement accounts (which surged in response). Moreover, real pretax interest rates rose sharply. Thus many point to the post-1981 period as one where the saving rate should have risen noticeably if saving is interest sensitive. However, the officially reported personal saving rate has plummeted from 7.3 percent of income in 1980-81 to about 4.4 percent in 1985-86, a decline of 40 percent. On this basis, Blinder (1985) and Hausman and Poterba (1986) conclude that personal saving is not interest sensitive.

This conclusion rests on two premises: the official savings rate is a reasonable measure of household saving and other forces were not deterring saving in the 1980s. Both presumptions are incorrect. Hendershott and Peek (1988) have examined the official computation of the saving rate and found it lacking for three reasons: (1) purchases of durable goods are treated as pure consumption, (2) contributions to government retirement plans are counted as government, not household, saving, and (3) the inflation-generated premium in interest rates, which simply compensates for expected capital losses on fixed-dollar financial assets, is included in household income. When Hendershott and Peek recompute the personal saving rate in the 1980s, it is flat, not plunging.

Moreover, the rise in the stock market between the summer of 1982 and the end of 1986 added over a trillion dollars to household wealth. Such an increase would be expected to reduce saving out of current income. The constancy of the personal saving rate, correctly measured, in the face of this wealth increase, suggests a positive response to the net return on saving. The 1981 expansion in retirement saving incentives may have stimulated household saving in spite of the observed decline in the official saving rate.

The 1986 Tax Act and Personal Saving

Numerous provisions in the 1986 Tax Act affect the return to saving. These include changes in tax rates on dividends, interest and capital gains, changes in the taxation of tax shelter activities, and changes in the deductibility of IRA and 401(k) retirement contributions. I first discuss the tax rate changes and attacks on tax shelters and then turn to the changed deductibility of retirement saving.

Table 4.1 contains marginal tax rates (federal plus net state and local) under both 1985 tax law and the Tax Act of 1986 for homeowners with different incomes in 1988 and different household status. The after-tax incomes are for households if they rented; if they owned they would have lower tax liabilities. The marginal tax rates are for owners and reflect substantial housing-related deductions; for renters the marginal rates would be higher. As can be seen, tax rates on marginal dividend and/or interest income are cut by 5 to 15 percentage points for married owners with incomes

Table 4.1
After-Tax Incomes as Renters and Marginal Tax Rates as Owners

Adjusted Gross 1988 Income	Married (2 Children)		Single		Household Head (With 1 Child)	
	1985 Law	1988 Law	1985 Law	1988 Law	1985 Law	1988 Law
12,500						
After-Tax Income	11,791	12,500	11,103	11,904	11,489	11,844
Marginal Tax Rate	.1420	'.0250	.1810	.1712	.1615	.1712
17,500						
After-Tax Income	15,919	16,344	14,936	15,144	15,457	15,894
Marginal Tax Rate	.1658	.1755	.2046	.1755	.1949	.1755
22,500						
After-Tax Income	19,950	20,368	18,711	18,834	19,403	19,918
Marginal Tax Rate	.1886	.1789	.2562	.3045	.2079	.1789
27,500						
After-Tax Income	23,799	24,377	22,303	22,182	23,183	23,927
Marginal Tax Rate	.2103	.1814	.2874	.3066	.2296	.1814
32,500						
After-Tax Income	27,572	28,448	25,839	25,653	26,903	27,660
Marginal Tax Rate	.2104	.1814	.2874	.3066	.2681	.1814
37,500						
After-Tax Income	31,306	32,521	29,321	29,181	30,475	31,083
Marginal Tax Rate	.2489	.1814	.3259	.3066	.2681	.3066
42,500						
After-Tax Income	34,891	35,898	32,526	32,670	33,862	34,446
Marginal Tax Rate	.2792	.1831	.3273	.3081	.3081	.3081
47,500						
After-Tax Income	38,450	39,272	35,685	36,167	37,213	37,979
Marginal Tax Rate	.2800	.3088	.3280	.3088	.3088	.3088
55,000						
After-Tax Income	43,473	44,435	40,339	41,102	42,109	43,245
Marginal Tax Rate	.3102	.3102	.4060	.3102	.3485	.3102
67,500						
After-Tax Income	51,506	53,160	47,636	49,265	49,743	51,970
Marginal Tax Rate	.3595	.3117	.4073	.3595	.3786	.3117
87,500						
After-Tax Income	63,919	67,088	58,803	62,484	61,556	65,335
Marginal Tax Rate	.4085	.3131	.4467	.3608	.4467	.3131
120,000						
After-Tax Income	83,428	88,561	76,613	84,278	80,143	86,808
Marginal Tax Rate	.4496	.3642	.5065	.3462	.4780	.3642

Source: Calculations performed by David Ling. For the assumptions underlying the calculations, see Hendershott and Ling (1986).

between $35,000 and $45,000 and above $65,000. For household heads and singles, respectively, such cuts occur for incomes above $50,000. This represents about 25 percent of married couples but only 10 percent of single and other household heads. Such rate declines tend to raise the after-tax return to savers. On the other hand, the statutory capital gains tax rate is increased by 8 to 15 percentage points for these same households.

Also acting to lower returns to savers are the anti-tax shelter provisions of the new law. For many years, different sources of income have been taxed differently under the federal tax code. For example, until 1981 "unearned" (nonlabor) income was subject to a far higher maximum tax rate than was "earned" or labor income. Also, capital gains have generally been taxed less heavily than other income, owing both to the gains exclusion and deferral until realization. Moreover, portfolio capital losses, while fully deductible against portfolio capital gains, have been deductible against only $3,000 of other income.

The 1986 Act introduces a new income class, passive income, with restrictions somewhat analogous to those on portfolio capital losses. Passive income is defined to include income generated from business and trade activities in which the taxpayer does not materially participate and from rental activities such as real estate. For individuals, partnerships, trusts, and personal service corporations, losses from passive activities can be used to offset income from other passive activities, but not other income (e.g., wages, interest, etc.). Losses that cannot be claimed in a particular year can be "banked" and used to offset passive income in future years.[3] Also, cumulative losses are deductible in full at the time of sale of the property, irrespective of whether a gain or loss is recognized.

The 1986 Act also strengthened the minimum tax considerably. Individuals must pay the higher of their regular tax liability or their minimum tax liability. Under the new law, the minimum tax liability is 21 percent (up from 20) of an individual's income base--regular taxable income plus specified tax preferences less a $40,000 exemption for married taxpayers ($30,000 for singles or individual filers). The exemption is reduced 25 cents for each dollar by which the income base exceeds $150,000; during this phaseout the effective tax rate is 26.5 percent.[4]

The 1986 Act expands the list of tax preferences to include accelerated depreciation on equipment (the difference between 200 percent declining balance and 150 percent declining balance), tax-exempt interest on new private activity bonds, and the appreciation component of charitable contributions. These expansions will increase the likelihood of taxpayers paying the minimum tax.

On net, the anti-shelter provisions and increase in capital gains taxation would appear to more than offset the decline in marginal tax rates on interest and dividends. These declines are significant for only the fifth of households with the highest incomes, and these households are just those most likely to have been using tax shelters and paying capital gains. The net return to saving is probably decreased.

The 1986 Act also reduces the tax advantages of retirement saving. IRA contributions for those with established pensions will no longer be deductible for households with incomes above $35,000 (singles) or $50,000 (married couples), and they will be only partially deductible for singles with incomes between $25,000 and $35,000 and marrieds with incomes between $40,000 and $50,000.[5] Also, the maximum deductible annual contributions to supplemental retirement accounts [401(k)s] has been lowered from $30,000 to $7,000. These changes certainly reduce the net return to savers, but many contend the reduction affects few on the margin. For high savers, IRA contributions are not the marginal dollars saved because the contributions are limited to $2000 a year. Moreover, previous saving can be transferred from taxable accounts to tax-exempt accounts.[6] Thus the surge in retirement contributions in the early 1980s (roughly $40 billion to IRAs and $20 billion to 401(k)'s in 1985 alone) may not have reflected an incentive-induced increase in saving, and removing these tax incentives may not reduce saving.

While these observations are relevant, a significant part of these contributions has likely affected behavior at the margin. Nearly 40 percent of IRA contributors made contributions below the maximum amount, and half of 401(k) contributions may have been by individuals contributing over the $7,000 limit (Hausman and Poterba, 1986). For these households, the reduced deductibility limits will lower the marginal return to saving.

Overall the marginal return to saving will decline. Higher taxation of returns on saving vehicles used by higher income households--IRAs, 401(k)s, real estate tax shelters and capital gains generally--will lower the net returns on these assets unless pretax returns rise sharply. In the absence of negative wealth effects of the tax changes, which would act to raise household saving, this saving will decline.

The 1986 Tax Act and Corporate and Foreign Saving

The effects on corporate and foreign saving are likely to be even more important than those on personal saving. The 1986 Act substantially increases the tax burden on corporations while lowering it on households. Over the 1987-92 period, the shift is $120 billion. This will certainly lower corporate saving, at least until pretax corporate returns rise to offset the impact on after-tax earnings. The issue is whether household saving will rise to offset the decline in corporate saving.

If the greater corporate taxation were on existing capital, then we would expect stock prices to decline and thus household wealth to fall. In response, households would increase their saving. This increase, plus the normal saving owing to the $120 billion increase in disposable income, would likely offset the decrease in corporate saving. However, under the 1986 Tax Act existing capital is taxed more favorably; Summers (1987) estimates that taxes on old capital will be $70 billion less in the 1987-91 period, while taxes on new capital will be $190 billion more. With old capital less heavily taxed, stock prices will rise, not fall, and household saving should be depressed as a result.[7]

An alternative analysis of the impact of the increase in corporate taxation on household saving asks whether households "pierce the corporate veil" without specifying the process through which this piercing occurs. Using official personal and corporate saving data, Hendershott and Peek (1988), like von Furstenburg (1981), find nearly a 50 percent offset, i.e., the coefficient of corporate saving in a personal saving equation is -0.43. However, both personal and corporate saving are mismeasured during inflationary periods, and the measurement errors are negatively correlated because households are net creditors and corporations are net debtors. When the saving series are corrected--when personal saving is lowered by the household inflation premium (and augmented by other adjustments) and corporate saving is raised by the corporate inflation premium, the coefficient of adjusted corporate saving switches to slightly positive. That is, changes in corporate saving do not affect household saving directly, but only indirectly through wealth changes. To illustrate, if existing capital were taxed less heavily, corporate saving and stock prices would both rise. The increase in stock prices would, through a wealth effect, lower household saving.

Finally, a word or two on foreign saving is appropriate. If interest rates tend to decline, as model simulations that assume constant national saving suggest they will, then the returns to foreign investors in the U.S. will decline (these investors do not pay U.S. taxes). As a result, foreign saving will decrease, the decline in interest rates will be dampened, and the U.S. capital stock will grow less rapidly. Krugman (1985) suggests that half of the potential rate decline would be offset by reduced foreign saving, and Summer's (1985) analysis is consistent with this.

INVESTMENT

Probably the most widely-cited economic benefit of tax reform is the efficiency gain from a better allocation of capital. The double taxation of corporate capital, the zero (or low) taxation of owner-occupied housing and state and local capital, the investment-credit bias in favor of equipment over structures, all lead to misallocations. A more efficient capital stock would be a more productive capital stock.

Potential Benefits

A major conclusion of the extensive research in recent years on efficiency is that the potential gains from a more efficient allocation of capital are not nearly as large as once thought. More specifically, the potential gains are probably less than one percent of GNP (Fullerton and Henderson, 1988). A simple example will illustrate why the gains are so small. Say that the economy has equal amounts of two types of capital with equal depreciation rates earning gross returns of 11 percent at the margin in one case and 9 percent in the other owing to a tax preference. A productivity gain can be achieved by equating returns in the two uses. Assuming Cobb-Douglas technology, roughly one-tenth of the currently tax-preferred capital earning between 9 and 10 percent would be shifted into the currently tax-discriminated capital. The shift is one-tenth because the marginal gross return is changing by one-tenth. The return on the shifted capital would rise from the 9 to 10 percent range to the 10 to 11 percent range. That is, the one-tenth of the capital stock reallocated would earn an additional percentage point. Thus, the initial 2 percentage point tax wedge reduced the <u>average</u> rate of return on the capital stock by only a tenth of a percentage point. With an average rate of return on the capital of 10 percent and an output/capital ratio below unity, the output gain is less than one percent.

This is not an unrealistic example. While net returns on specific types of capital under old tax law may have differed by as much as four percentage points (as shown in Table 4.2), the average net returns on the higher-earning half of the capital stock was less than two percentage points more than that on the lower-earning half.

A second source of productivity enhancement is an increase in the rate of business investment owing to either greater total investment or a reallocation of a given investment level from housing to business outlays. Here, the potential output gains are more substantial.

Summers (1981b) provides some illustrative computations, again assuming Cobb-Douglas technology. With exogenous technological growth, an increase in the share of output devoted to net business investment would temporarily raise the rate of productivity growth as the economy moves to a higher output level. Eventually, though, a new output/capital ratio will be achieved, and the rate of growth of output and capital will return to the long-run rate given by the growth rates of labor supply and technology. With a one-third increase in the business-investment share of output, the productivity growth rate increases by only 0.1 percent per year in the first decade and lesser amounts thereafter. The long-run output path, however, is 7 1/2 percent higher.[8] If instead technological progress is embodied in capital goods, the same increase in investment has a larger short-run impact because it accelerates the introduction of new technology. The increase in the productivity growth rate is nearly 0.2 percent per year during the first decade. However, the long-run output path is not any higher; the economy just gets there quicker (Phelps, 1962).

This output gain is not free. If an increase in saving is the source of the greater business investment, then consumption is reduced during the transition to the new equilibrium. If reduced housing investment is the source, then the consumption-of-housing-services path is lower forever.

1986 Tax Act

The Tax Reform Act of 1986 has negative direct implications for virtually every type of capital good. Longer depreciation lives raise the investment hurdle rates (annual rental costs) for all structures except owner-occupied housing, the elimination of investment tax credits increases hurdle rates for equipment and public utility structures, the decrease in the corporate tax rate increases the hurdle rate for intangible capital (advertising and research and development), and the cut in personal tax rates lowers the demand for owner-occupied housing. Only inventories (and land) are unaffected. With the demand for all investment goods either falling or being unchanged, interest rates will certainly decline. The magnitude of the decline depends on the interest sensitivities of both the supply of domestic and foreign saving and of investment demand itself. Hendershott (1987) constructed a model in which total saving is independent of rates of return and the demands for capital are approximately unitary elastic with respect to the rental prices of capital goods. In this model, interest rates have to decline by well over a percentage point to offset the negative capital provisions of the Act. That is, rates have to decline by this much to maintain the aggregate demand for capital at its pre-reform level.[9]

Of course, interest rates will decline less if the supply of saving is reduced, and a reduction should be anticipated. As discussed above, a decline in private saving should be expected owing to the reduction in retirement saving incentives and the shift of the tax burden from low saving households to higher saving corporations. Moreover, a tendency toward lower interest rates will be mitigated by decreased foreign saving.

Figure 4.1 illustrates the general impact of the Tax Act on interest rates (i) and net investment, both business (BUS) and the sum of business and other (SUM). The downward sloping solid schedules, BUS and SUM, are net investment demands under old law, and the solid SAV schedule is net saving under old law. For convenience SAV is drawn vertically. The level of net

Impact of 1986 Tax Act on Interest Rates and Net Investment Flows

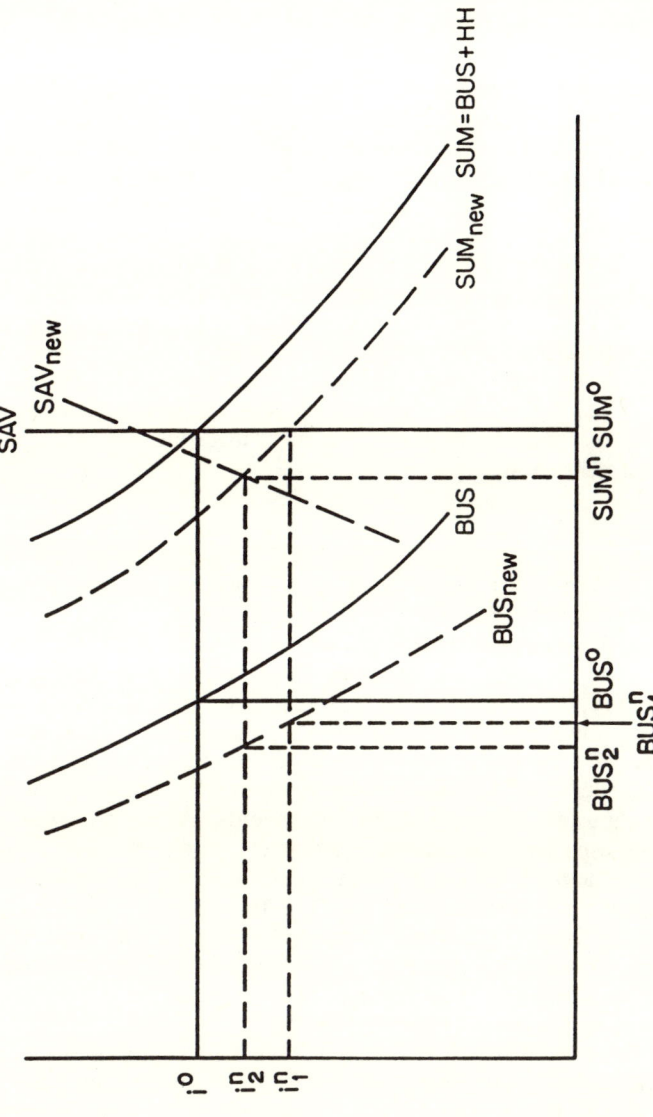

Figure 4.1

investment and net saving is SUM^0, the business component of investment is BUS^0, and the interest rate level is i^0.

The 1986 Tax Act shifts the SUM and BUS schedules leftward to SUM_{new} and BUS_{new}. If net saving were unchanged, i would decline to i_1^n, and $BUS_1^0 - BUS_1^n$ would be reallocated from business to other investment under the assumption that the Tax Act disfavors business investment more than other investment. Model simulations (see below) generally give estimates of this decline in rates and reallocation of investment. If, however, net saving is positively related to interest rates, owing either to domestic or foreign behavior, and the domestic component of saving shifts leftward (as argued above), then the net saving schedule under the 1986 Tax Act becomes SAV_{new}. The leftward shift and positive slope cushion the decline in interest rates to i_2^n, increase the decline in business investment to BUS_2^n, and lower total investment to SUM^n.

Hendershott

Table 4.2 contains estimates of the changes in investment incentives contained in the 1986 Tax Act. The first column reports net (of depreciation) pretax required annual returns (investment hurdle rates) for a variety of corporate and noncorporate investments under 1985 law. The next two pairs of columns report estimated changes in these returns under two assumptions regarding tax-induced changes in interest rates, a percentage point decline and no change (the appendix contains the specifics of these calculations). As can be seen, under 1985 tax law the especially tax-favored assets were owner-occupied housing of high-income households, equipment, and intangible capital; the especially tax-disadvantaged assets were corporate inventories and industrial structures. The investment tax credit gave equipment its advantage, the expense of advertising and R&D outlays accounts for the intangible advantage, and the nontaxation of owner housing returns explains that large advantage for high tax bracket households. Corporate investments are generally disfavored by their "double" taxation--taxation at both the business (corporate) and investor (personal) levels.

The 1986 Tax Act is effective in reducing disparities among hurdle rates within each broad sector. In every case, the hurdle rate of the previously most tax-favored asset rises the most (equipment and owned housing of high-

Table 4.2: Net Pretax Required Rates of Return (%)

	1985	1986 Constant Real After Tax	1986 Constant Nominal	Change Constant Real After Tax	Change Constant Nominal	Change of Fullerton Henderson and Mackie
Corporate Investments						
Inventories	6.8	5.9	6.9	-0.9	0.1	-1.3/-0.03
Structures	6.1	5.9	6.9	-0.2	0.8	0.1/0.6
Utility Structures	5.0	6.1	7.1	1.1	2.1	1.0/1.5
Intangibles	3.8	3.8	4.4	0.0	0.6	
Equipment	3.4	5.6	6.5	2.2	3.1	2.3/2.7
Average (excl. intangibles)*	5.0	5.9	6.9	0.9	1.9	
Noncorporate Investments						
Inventories	5.2	4.3	5.1	-0.9	-0.1	-0.2
Commercial Structures	4.6	4.7	5.6	0.1	1.0	0.2
Residential Structures	4.3	4.6	5.5	0.3	1.2	0.2
Intangibles	2.8	2.8	3.4	0.0	0.6	
Equipment	2.2	4.4	5.2	2.2	3.0	2.3
Average (excl. intangibles)*	4.1	4.6	5.5	0.5	1.4	
Owner-Occupied Housing						
Income (000 of 1986$) — Marginal Tax Rates 1985 1986						
13-25 .166 .176	4.7	3.8	4.6	-0.9	-0.1	
25-30 .187 .180	4.5	3.7	4.5	-0.8	0.0	
30-50 .251 .184	3.9	3.7	4.5	-0.2	0.6	
50-100 .364 .316	2.9	2.6	3.3	-0.3	0.4	
100-200 .455 .370	2.1	2.3	2.9	0.2	0.8	
Average	3.5	3.2	3.9	-0.3	0.4	0.1
Change in Nominal Interest Rate		-1.0	0.0	-1.0	0.0	-0.3

*Intangibles are not included in the average because no data exist (or could even be approximated) on the stock of intangible capital (see Fullerton and Lyons, 1987).

income households) and that of the least tax-favored asset falls or rises the least (inventories and owned housing of low-income households). In fact, the investment hurdle rates for business capital under the 1986 Act are remarkably close, except for intangible capital. In contrast, the Tax Act is
perverse in terms of sectors. Hurdle rates for the most heavily taxed corporate sector are increased the most, while those for the least heavily taxed sector, owner-occupied housing, decrease or increase the least. According to my calculations, the losses from less equal treatment of sectors exceed the gains from more equal treatment of assets.

Fullerton, Henderson and Mackie

Fullerton, Henderson and Mackie (1987) have made comparable calculations using a far more detailed general equilibrium model. The model contains 15 consumer goods produced by 19 producers' goods which, in turn, have labor and 38 types of both corporate and noncorporate capital as inputs. The 38 capital goods include 20 types of equipment, 5 utility structures, 10 other structures, inventories, and 2 types of land. In contrast, all owner housing is presumed to be held by a single, average tax-bracket household.

The Fullerton-Henderson-Mackie (FHM) model gives results remarkably similar to my simple model. Their average changes in hurdle rates for the investment aggregates under two model specifications for corporations are listed in column 4 of Table 4.2. The changes are generally in between those in columns 2 and 3, which is just as expected because their calculations presume a 30 basis point decline in interest rates.

The FHM model simulation actually computes a 60 basis point interest rate decline to maintain the aggregate demand for capital. Most of the difference between this and my larger estimated decline stems from their inclusion of land. Land constitutes 60 percent of noncorporate capital and 30 percent of all capital. Because land is not taxed more heavily under the 1986 Tax Act, including land in the model as an elastically supplied good greatly dampens the interest rate decline needed to maintain the aggregate demand for capital.

The inclusion of land is also important to FHM's capital stock and efficiency results. With no saving response, corporate capital decreases by 8 percent, noncorporate-nonhousing capital increases by 7 percent, and housing rises by 2 percent. Noncorporate capital rises because most land is in this sector and the demand for land rises absolutely when interest rates decline. With land excluded, corporate and noncorporate-nonhousing capital decrease by 10 percent and 2 percent, respectively, giving a decline in total business capital of 8 percent.

If one views nonland business capital as the key total capital variable because one does not accept the assumption that land is as easily produced as plant and equipment (or because new technology is not embodied in land), then the Tax Act has a significantly negative effect. The decline in business capital, and thus the negative impact of the Tax Act, will be magnified by the anticipated decreases in private and foreign saving.

Fullerton, Henderson and Mackie find that the efficiency gains from better asset allocation within sectors outweigh the greater losses from poorer sectoral allocation.[10] One might expect the far more detailed asset treatment to lead to such a result if different classes of equipment or of structures were taxed far more differently under old law than new. In fact, though, different classes were not taxed all that differently under old law and do not seem to be taxed more evenly under the 1986 Tax Act (compare the differences in effective tax rates in FHM, Table 3). The greater FHM gains come from the inclusion of land which, with inventories, was the heaviest taxed asset under old law and is about averaged-taxed under the new 1986 Act.[11]

Galper, Lucke and Toder

Galper, Lucke and Toder (GLT) take an approach nearly opposite to FHM. GLT emphasize financial behavior, risk taking, and taxation at the personal, rather than, business level. All housing is assumed to be owner-occupied, and it and consumer durables are held by 400 different households, differentiated by income, wealth, marital and itemization status. In contrast only, single, conglomerated corporate and noncorporate business capital stocks, rather than 38 classes, are analyzed.

The GLT model computes a percentage point decline in interest rates to maintain the aggregate demand for capital. The major capital stock changes are a 12 percent decrease in state and local government capital and a roughly offsetting, in dollar amounts, 6 percent increase in consumer durables, two assets not included in the FHM model. Corporate and noncorporate capital each decline by a single percentage point. These declines could rise to as much as 5 percent when a decline in private saving and an endogenous fall in foreign saving in response to the decline in interest rates are incorporated.

Summary

All three models suggest five to ten percent declines in business investment. A ten percent decline, lowering the share of net business investment in net output from 0.045 to 0.04, would, from the growth calculations discussed earlier, lower the long-run output path by three percent.

CONCLUSION

The Tax Reform Act of 1986 will lower the share of net output channeled into net investment and will tilt net investment from industrial to other uses. Both effects will reduce the long-run output path. On the other hand, the industrial investment made will be marginally more efficient. Labor supply will be largely unaffected. On net, the long-run output path will be reduced by two to four percent, and productivity growth will slow until this lower path is reached. That legislation shifting the tax burden from labor and existing capital to new investment would have this result should hardly come as a surprise.

Let me expand briefly on these conclusions. Interest and dividend income is generally taxed at a lower rate. On the other hand, capital gains are taxed more heavily, tax shelters are restricted (new passive loss rules and a more inclusive minimum income tax base), and deductible contributions to retirement plans are reduced. On net, the incentive for households to save will almost certainly be reduced in the aggregate. The reduction will be magnified, at least in the short run, by the general shift in tax payments from households, with low saving rates, to businesses, with higher saving rates.

The reduction in investment incentives and cuts in tax rates will lower demands for most capital goods (equipment, structures, and intangibles) and will leave unchanged demands for the rest (inventories and land). Because the demand for investment funds will decrease more than the supply, interest rates will decline, although reductions in foreign saving in response to the rate-decline will cushion it. The result will be less net investment and a smaller share of it devoted to the industrial sector. The industrial investment will be marginally more efficient, but its increased quality will not balance the decreased quantity.

Labor income is generally taxed less heavily. The reduction in statutory tax rates is financed by disallowing household income-tax deductions (e.g., sales taxes and retirement contributions), by taxing tax shelters more heavily, and by reducing business investment incentives. All of these increase the net-of-tax price of either current or future consumption. Thus, while the after-tax wage rate is higher, so are prices of goods. Because the Tax Act is revenue neutral, and, if anything, increases the progressivity of the tax system, there is no reason to believe the quantity of goods workers can purchase with an extra hour's effort will increase or that labor supply will expand. In fact, the reverse could occur.

How might growth advocates reasonably respond to the 1986 Tax Act? A simple (intellectually, not politically) response would be to reverse the Act--unpass it. But this would reverse a number of beneficial aspects of the law. The expansion of the standard deduction and personal exemption are widely viewed as increasing fairness, and the cut in marginal personal tax rates has many obvious advantages: remaining tax preferences will be worth less, the consumer durables and housing stocks will be allocated more efficiently among households (GLT, 1988), the taxation of capital income will be less sensitive to inflation (Henderson, 1986), and risk will be borne more efficiently (GLT, 1988). Keeping the enlarged standard deductions and personal exemptions and maintaining at least most of the lower/flatter tax rate schedule seems highly desirable.[12] What then should be done to increase saving and ensure that it is channelled into industrial capital?

Within the given constraints, a growth policy would be the following. First, additional tax revenues need to be raised, either by increasing all tax rates a few points or introducing a new consumption tax.[13] Second, part of the revenues should be earmarked to reduce the federal deficit (increase national saving) and part should be used to reintroduce business investment incentives to ensure that most of the increased national saving flows into business investment, rather than being offset by a decline in foreign saving or being diverted into other capital. An investment tax credit, which could be applied to plant as well as equipment, would be preferred to reaccelerating depreciation because the latter would encourage nonproductive tax-motivated trading of assets.

Notes

1. Data for 1959-79 are contained in the 1982 Economic Report of the President, Table 5-1, p. 113. The data pertain to private nonfarm nonhousing GNP.

2. Bosworth (1984) contains a useful discussion of many of the general topics addressed in this paper.

3. An exception applies to "small landlords." Taxpayers who actively manage residential rental investments may deduct up to $25,000 in losses against nonpassive income if their adjusted gross income computed without regard to the losses is less than $100,000. This amount is phased out one dollar for two dollars of income for taxpayers with incomes above $100,000 so that no losses are allowed for anyone who earns above $150,000.

4. For a detailed discussion of both the individual and corporate minimum taxes, see Graetz and Sunley (1988).

5. At an 8 percent interest rate and a 25 year investment horizon, elimination of the deductibility, but continuation of the tax deferral on interest earned, removes half of the tax benefit.

6. Venti and Wise (1987) estimate that only 20 percent of contributions constitute transfers of assets.

7. Downs and Hendershott (1987) estimate that the stock market should have increased by 10 to 15 percent.

8. The output-labor ratio equals $(s/n)\exp[(1-a)/a]$, where s is the fraction of net output devoted to net investment, n is the rate of growth in labor, and a is the elasticity of output with respect to labor (Solow, 1956). The ratio of new output (based on s^*) to old output is then $(s^*/s)\exp[(1-a)/a]$. With $s = 0.045$, $s^* = 0.06$, and $a = 0.8$, the ratio is 1.075.

9.   Much of the rate decline should have occurred prior to enactment of the Tax Act. All tax reform plans considered in 1986 proposed elimination of the investment tax credit for equipment and public utility structures <u>retroactive</u> to the beginning of 1986, and the likelihood of some version of tax reform passing was high virtually all year. Thus the decline in interest rates and the weakness in equipment expenditures experienced in 1986 was partially attributable to the anticipated removal of this provision. Indeed, half of the model-calculated decline in interest rates is due solely to the elimination of this credit.

10.   Their analysis (like Hendershott's) does not include intangible capital and does not reflect the negative impact of the various accounting and specific industry rule changes on investment demand. Inclusion of tangible capital and incorporation of these other impacts could easily reverse the FHM results.

11.   It is worth noting that both the FHM gain and Hendershott loss are small; the difference is important only when an undue emphasis is placed on the sign of the efficiency change.

12.   I would view extension of the current maximum rate of 33 percent to the highest income, or even a maximum rate of 35 percent at very high incomes, as being consistent with maintaining the lower schedule.

13.   Needless to say, most everyone would prefer to generate the increase in government saving by cutting spending. I will not burden the reader with my preferred spending cuts.

Bibliography

Aaron, Henry J., "The Impossible Dream Comes True," in Pechman (ed.) Tax Reform and the U.S. Economy, The Brookings Institution, Washington, D.C., 1987.

Blinder, Alan, "Discussion," in Economic Consequences of Tax Simplification, Federal Reserve Bank of Boston, 1985, 92-98.

Boskin, Michael J., "Taxation, Saving, and the Rate of Interest," Journal of Political Economy, April 1978, 86, S3-S27.

Bosworth, Barry P., Tax Incentives and Economic Growth, The Brookings Institution, Washington, D.C., 1984.

Browning, Edgar K. and Jacquelene M., "Why Not a True Flat Rate Tax?," Cato Journal, Fall 1985, 5, 629-50.

Downs, Thomas and Hendershott, Patric H., "Tax Policy and Stock Prices," National Tax Journal, June 1987, 183-190.

Evans, Owen J., "Tax Policy, the Interest Elasticity of Saving, and Capital Accumulation," American Economic Review, June 1983, 91, 249-265.

Fullerton, Don, Yolanda K. Henderson, and James Mackie, "Investment Allocation and Growth Under the Tax Reform Act of 1986," Compendium of Tax Research 1987, Office of Tax Analysis, Department of Treasury, Washington, D.C., 1987.

Fullerton, Don and Yolanda K. Henderson, "A Disaggregate Equilibrium Model of the Tax Distortions Among Assets, Sectors, and Industries," International Economic Review, 1988.

Fullerton, Don and Andrew B. Lyon, "Tax Neutrality and Tangible Capital," in Summers (ed.) Tax Policy and the Economy, NBER Conference Report, 1987, 57-103.

Galper, Harvey, Robert Lucke and Eric Toder, "The Economic Effects of Tax Reform: A General Equilibrium Analysis," in Aaron, Galper and

Pechman (eds.) Uneasy Compromise: Problems of a Hybrid Income-Consumption Tax, Brookings Institution, forthcoming 1988.

Hall, Robert E., "Consumption and Real Interest Rates," NBER Working Paper No. 1694, Cambridge, MA, 1985.

Hausman, Jerry A. and James M. Poterba, "Household Behavior and the Tax Reform Act of 1986," NBER Working Paper No. 2120. Cambridge, MA, 1987.

Henderson, Yolanda, "Lessons from Federal Reform of Business Taxes," New England Economic Review, November/December 1986, 9-25.

Hendershott, Patric H., "Tax Changes and Capital Allocation in the 1980s," in Feldstein (ed.) The Effects of Taxation on Capital Accumulation, Chicago: University of Chicago Press, 1987, 259-90.

Hendershott, Patric H., and David C. Ling, "Likely Impacts of the Administration Proposal and HR3838," in Follain (ed.), Tax Reform and Real Estate, The Urban Institute, 1986, 87-112.

Hendershott, Patric H., and Joe Peek, "Private Saving in the United States: 1950-85," in Lipsey and Tice (eds.), Measurement of Saving, Investment and Wealth, NBER Income and Wealth volume, forthcoming 1988.

Krugman, Paul R., "Fiscal Policy, Interest Rates, and Exchange Rates: Some Simple Analytics," MIT Working Paper 391, Cambridge, MA, 1985.

Lea, Michael, "Housing and Capital Markets," mimeo, January 1988.

Phelps, Edmund S., "The New View of Investment: A NeoClassical Analysis," Quarterly Journal of Economics, November 1962, 76, 548-67.

Slemrod, Joel, "Can a Revenue-Neutral, Distributionally-Neutral Tax Reform Increase Labor Supply?," mimeo, July 1987.

Solow, Robert, "A Contribution to Economic Growth," Quarterly Journal of Economics, February 1956, 70, 65-94.

Summers, Lawrence H., "A Fair Tax Act That's Bad for Business," Harvard Business Review, March-April 1987, 53-59.

___, "Tax Policy and Corporate Investment," in Meyer (ed.), The Supply-Side Effects of Economic Policy, Center for the Study of American Business, 1981, 115-148.

___, "Capital Taxation and Accumulation in a Life Cycle Growth Model," American Economic Review, September 1981, 533-544.

___, "Issues in National Savings Policy," NBER Working Paper No. 1710, 1985.

Venti, Steven F. and David A. Wise, "IRAs and Saving," in Feldstein (ed.), The Effects of Taxation on Capital Accumulation, Chicago: University of Chicago Press, 1987, 7-48.

von Furstenberg, George M., "Saving," in Aaron and Pechman, How Taxes Affect Economic Behavior, Studies of Government Finance, The Brookings Institution, Washington, D.C., 1981, 327-402.

APPENDIX: THE CALCULATION OF PRETAX REQUIRED RETURNS

The decision to invest depends on whether the present value of the expected revenue from investment, net of direct operating expenses and indirect taxes, exceeds the outlay on the investment. On marginal investments, the present value will equal the outlay. Put another way, in the absence of taxes, the net operating income from an investment must cover the real interest rate plus depreciation. After allowance for taxation, the equilibrium condition for investment is

$$\rho = (r+d)\frac{1 - k - \tau z}{1 - \tau} \qquad (1)$$

where ρ is the marginal product of capital (initial net operating income), r is the real after-tax financing rate, d is the economic depreciation rate, k is the investment tax credit, τ is the business tax rate, and z is the present value of tax depreciation allowances. The right side of equation (1) is the "investment hurdle rate" for a particular asset. The lower the hurdle rate, the greater will be production of the asset and the lower will be the productivity of the marginal investment (ρ). In a "neutral" tax system, ρ-d would be the same for all assets. That is, the net marginal productivity of all investments would be equal at the margin.

The real after-tax financing rate (r) depoends on the pre-tax debt rate, the rate at which interest is deductible, the required return on equity (which depends on capital gains taxation), the loan-to-value ratio, and the inflation rate. In general, r is higher for industrial (corporate) structures than for noncorporate real estate because the required equity rate is higher owing to the double taxation of dividends. For noncorporate structures I assume a real after-tax interest rate of 0.0275 both before and after tax reform (the cut in tax rates tends to raise r but a decline in pretax interest rates lowers r); a real rate of 0.0375 is assumed for corporate investments.

The present value of tax depreciation, in the absence of trading, is simply the tax depreciation stream, with the basis adjusted for the tax credit received, discounted by nominal after-tax interest rates:

$$z = (1-kB) \sum_{t=1}^{L} \frac{TAXD_t}{[(1+r)(1+\pi)]^t}, \qquad (2)$$

where B is the fraction of the tax credit by which the basis is reduced, $TAXD_t$ is the depreciation in year t, and π is the expected inflation rate, assumed to be 0.045. Tax-based trading will occur if the tax benefits from the trade, τz, exceed the costs of reestablishing the depreciable base, $\beta + \tau_{cg}$, where β is the selling cost and τ_{cg} is the statutory capital gains tax. More formally, if trading every J periods (J $\geq$ L) is advantageous, up to T trades, the present value of tax depreciation becomes

$$z' = z + [z-(\beta+\tau_{cg})/\tau] \sum_{j=1}^{T} [(1-d)/(1-r)]^{jJ}. \qquad (2')$$

As it turns out, trading was advantageous under 1985 law but will not be under the Tax Reform Act of 1986.

In this analysis, we assume that the marginal tax rate of the marginal investor was 0.45 (including state and local income taxes) under old law and 0.36 under new. The 0.0275 real rate and 0.045 expected inflation rate are consistent with a 0.09 percent risk-free interest rate and a 0.023 percent risk premium under old law and a 0.08 percent risk-free rate under new law. With no decline in interest rates, the real rate is raised by (1-.36).01 to 0.0339 (0.0439 for corporations).

For owner-occupied housing, the τ's in equation (1) are zero (imputed rents are not taxed and no depreciation is deductible for tax purposes). Moreover, the real after-tax financing rate and the value of property tax deductions vary with the household's tax bracket. To make the analysis comparable to that of depreciable properties, we compute the net (of depreciation) marginal product for owner-occupied housing as

$$\rho\text{-d} = (1-\tau)(i-.005) + p - \pi - \tau\tau_p$$
$$= i + p - \pi - \tau(i+\tau_p) - (1-\tau).005 \qquad (3)$$

where i is the nominal debt rate, p is the risk premium, π is the expected inflation rate, τ_p is the property tax rate, and the $(1-\tau).005$ is the interest rate subsidy received by households with incomes under $100,000 because of mortgage pass-through programs of the Federal agencies (Lea, 1988). The same p and π values are used as above, and τ_p is set equal to 0.012. Net required pretax returns (ρ-d) are reported in Table IV.2 of the text for a variety of assets both before and after the 1986 Tax Act.

COMMENT

Emil J. Sunley

Economics has long been called the "dismal science." Patric Hendershott clearly is a practitioner of this science for he paints a dismal picture of the Tax Reform Act of 1986. The Act will lower the share of net output channeled into net investment and will tilt net investment from industrial to other uses. Although individual marginal tax rates are lowered, labor supply will largely be unaffected. He concludes that Congress should unpass the 1986 Act.

Pat's paper contains much that technically is quite good. Yet in spite of the strong technical aspects of this paper, I believe that his conclusions regarding the 1986 Act are too negative. There is much that is good in this legislation. By leveling the playing field between tax favored and fully-taxed investments and activities, the Act will reduce the importance of taxes when making decisions on how to earn income, how to invest, and what to consume.

Let me make two specific comments on the paper. First, Pat concludes his paper by recommending that if additional tax revenues are needed, they should be obtained by taxing consumption. A distributionally neutral consumption tax would have a greater distortion on labor supply than an income tax because marginal tax rates will have to be higher on the smaller consumption tax base to achieve the same degree of progressivity as under the income tax. Shifting from income to consumption taxes may increase savings and investment, but it surely would have a more adverse effect on labor supply than the 1986 Act.

Second, in his discussion of savings effects, Hendershott maintains that the tighter limits on tax shelters enacted as part of the 1986 Act will reduce savings. Pat, however, does not mention that the new tax shelter rules will improve the allocation of investment. Neither of the two equilibrium models discussed in the paper (the Fullerton, Henderson, and Mackie model or the Galper, Lucke, and Toder model) are able to take into account the new tax shelter rules. These models underestimate the improvement in the allocation of investment that will follow from the 1986 Act.

Pat concludes his paper with some very sweeping recommendations. First, if additional tax revenues are needed, they should be raised by taxing consumption. Second, some of the additional revenues should be earmarked to reduce the Federal deficit. Third, the rest of the revenues should be used to reintroduce business investment incentives.

The tax challenge for the 1990's will be to raise additional Federal revenues. To bring the gap between Federal spending and revenues down to an acceptable level, tax increases, along with both domestic and defense spending reductions, will be needed. On the tax side, the critical issue will be whether the increased revenue should come through greater reliance on the income tax--either additional tax base broadening or an increase in marginal tax rates--or from a major new Federal consumption tax such as the value added tax, which is essentially a sales tax collected at every stage of production and distribution. This clearly will be the watershed issue for our tax system.

The question of whether the Government should be given a new weapon for the tax arsenal is not just an economic question which can be analyzed in terms of labor supply, investment, and savings effects. There are important issues of political economy that are difficult to quantify.

The most critical issue is how the additional revenues will be used. Pat supports a new consumption tax and recommends that the revenues be used for deficit reduction and restoring investment incentives. Others who support a consumption tax want the revenues to be used for deficit reduction and new social programs such as a Government sponsored program for long-term care for the elderly.

The opposition to a consumption tax will be fierce and also divided. Some will oppose a consumption tax because they fear it is too regressive. Others fear that a new consumption tax, such as a VAT, would be a money machine.

If the value added tax is rejected in favor of heavier increased use of the income tax, it will partly be because we as a nation have decided that we prefer the tax evils we know to the tax evils we know not. If, instead, a value added tax is enacted, it will only be done after the Administration and Congress have rejected all the available alternatives.

5 A BUSINESSMAN'S PERSPECTIVE ON COMPETITIVENESS

Paul J. Rizzo

Ladies and gentlemen, it's a pleasure and honor to be here today with this illustrious group.

I assume you all read and hear a great deal about budget deficits, exchange rates, and protectionism. There are enough experts on both sides of these issues to make all our politicians happy!

You have also heard a great deal about "competitiveness" of the American economy as a whole -- competitiveness of particular industries -- autos, steel, textiles, chemicals, electronics, etc.!

What I would like to do is give you one more businessman's perspective on this subject.

Former Deputy Treasury Secretary Dick Darman made some rather acerbic comments recently regarding businessmen who spend less time on their R & D budgets than on their golf scores, and can't be reached before 10:00 or after 4:00 unless you have the number of their car telephone.

In looking at the schedule you have for today, he obviously couldn't be talking about you. You not only have a full morning and afternoon, you even have a working lunch! It is probably only appropriate that you have a busy day to set an example for all of us in these days of questionable U.S. competitiveness -- a subject on which I want to share a few thoughts.

There is little question that recent exchange rates are helping American business enormously in achieving cost parity--or better--with our trading partners. While we now can expect to be more price competitive, the issue of competitiveness goes far beyond cost and price.

First, you can rest assured that our foreign competitors are going to concentrate on cost reduction, and we will hardly see prices rise proportionate to exchange rate fluctuation.

Also, there can be little doubt that quality, design, technology and marketing are all issues that will not be neglected by our competitors. And while competitive price is an important factor, it's hardly the most desirable competitive strategy.

Hopefully, we will not assume that our problems are so simple that the dollar devaluation alone is the total solution. Nothing could be further from the truth.

We are all painfully aware that the USA is no longer the dominant world economic power. At best we are on a par. Gone are the days of the "ugly American"; now we must deal with the "humble American" who has a crisis of self-confidence. This may be the first sign of progress.

Now that we Americans have recovered from the shock of not being invincible, and as we have learned to recognize the importance of quality, design, technology and customer service, as well as price, it's useful to reflect upon some of the fundamentals that have changed the international competitive environment over the past decade -- fundamentals that are probably continuing to change and will impact future returns on current investments.

First, it's important to recognize that the developed world is rapidly becoming a very homogeneous marketplace -- with almost instantaneous distribution of any new innovation. Judging from the similarity among the youth of Asia, Europe and the USA, this trend can be expected to accelerate. One may suspect that there may be more similarities among youth in different countries than between generations in the same country. I am thinking of clothes, music, computers, autos -- youth is the same around the world!

I personally believe this may have very significant strategic implications when coupled with other changing factors. For example, technological lead time is rapidly shrinking. Also, there are many effective competitors with comparable technological capability. The result is that you can no longer move serially from one market to another hoping you will beat your competitor to market -- it will not happen in today's world market. Time between invention, manufacture and distribution has shrunk significantly in the last decade. When coupled with world-wide simultaneous distribution, time assumes a new competitive dimension.

This phenomenon alone would seem to place an incredible premium on world-wide distribution. Kenichi Ohmae of McKinsey and Co. calls this the Anchorage perspective -- Anchorage being 7 hours by jet from Europe, the USA and Japan.

Another fundamental that seems very different is capital intensity. We all know that manufacturing employment has been declining, so it should not be a surprise that direct labor, as a manufacturing cost element, has been diminishing for decades and is expected to continue to do so.

A semi-conductor manufacturing line could be built in the 50's and 60's for $5-$10 million. Today it's $300 million. Labor content was more than 25% ten years ago -- today it's less than 5%.

In the auto industry Nissan's direct labor is 7% of cost; Toyota's direct labor is 6% of cost.

Japan produces 13 million autos a year with 670,000 people -- including suppliers. By contrast GM has 690,000 employees. Toyota held manpower steady at 45,000 while output has increased 3.5 times in the last decade. The good news is, the U.S. auto industry is well down that path -- the bad news is, they are a little behind.

So what are the implications? First, significant up-front investment dictates that we get to market broadly and quickly. Volume is critical to success -- because of the high fixed cost. In this case, volume equals productivity.

While manufacturing labor cost is declining, I am not suggesting that it is in any way less important. Human resources are more important than ever. In an increasingly complex facility that all competitors also have, management and technicians are the one variable that makes the difference. It's no longer a cost management problem because the costs are relatively fixed. The issues are volume, quality, logistics, flexibility. So, ironically, the fewer the people, the more important each one becomes. Enlightened labor relations are absolutely critical.

Thus, it would also seem apparent that high front-end investment dictates as broad a market as possible -- reached as rapidly as possible. Thus, the significance of world-wide distribution. You can be sure that this is what your competitor is doing. These characteristics apply to steel, chemicals, textiles, electronics as well as autos.

This phenomenon is not limited to manufacturing -- it is also important to examine the changing investment requirements for many service industries -- investment banking and commercial banking for example, and the travel industry, are merely two examples where some of the same dynamics appear.

It is important to recognize that in addition to the increasing capital intensity of manufacturing, the whole technological cycle is accelerating. Not only are there more technologically capable competitors in each industry, the rate at which inventions and innovations find their way to market has dramatically increased.

Semiconductors, computers, consumer electronics, autos, cameras, and I believe the list is endless, continue to demonstrate rapid technological change across a broad range of competitors -- world-wide.

Obviously, this process requires a very capable technical organization -- which in itself represents a fixed cost that adds to the necessity for rapid world-wide distribution.

In looking back over the past decade, industry-by-industry, I think it's apparent why the concept of a national industrial policy -- which a few years ago was strongly advocated in some circles -- is an idea whose time has gone! The hi-tech industries of 5 years ago do not appear to be in any way exempt from the international competitive marketplace. In 1986 the USA ran a deficit in electronics. Simultaneously, many of the so-called smokestack industries -- i.e., autos, steel, textiles -- assume many so-called hi-tech characteristics -- in manufacturing process, if not in product delivered to the market. So today's hi-tech may be tomorrow's lo-tech -- and vice versa. So, classifying industries as hi-tech or lo-tech hardly seems useful.

As I said, it's popular these days, when we think of international competitiveness, to think in terms of cost, quality, technology and it will be a rare enterprise indeed that succeeds without addressing these issues -- internationally.

However, other very significant fundamentals in the competitive environment that we faced in the business world 20 years ago have changed dramatically. At this point it is important to recognize that the environment -- everywhere -- will continue to be dynamic if not volatile; the fundamental competitive issues we need to address are organization structures, distribution channels, and human resources. The winners in this new game will build organizations with the capability, perspective, and motivation, to continually adjust to an ever-changing marketplace. I guess that means I subscribe to Tom Peters' new theory "Thriving on Chaos."

Frankly, I believe the vast majority of American business executives understand this very well. Maybe it has taken us longer than we would like, but I am encouraged that the private sector has finally recognized that many of our traditional management practices are no longer valid.

My parting suggestion is -- never relax. When things appear to be going well, assume you are wrong -- because you are probably missing something!